GLENCOE

Writing
for the Workplace

Nan Merrick Phifer

**Glencoe
McGraw-Hill**

New York, New York   Columbus, Ohio   Woodland Hills, California   Peoria, Illinois

REVIEWERS

Glencoe/McGraw-Hill

A Division of The **McGraw·Hill** *Companies*

Copyright © 1999 by the McGraw-Hill Companies, Inc. All rights reserved. Except
as permitted under the United States Copyright Act, no part of this publication may
be reproduced or distributed in any form or by any means, or stored in a database
or retrieval system, without prior written permission of the publisher.

Send all inquiries to:

Glencoe/McGraw-Hill
936 Eastwind Drive
Westerville, OH 43081

Text: ISBN: 0-02-804181-X
Instructor's Manual: ISBN: 0-02-804182-8

Printed in the United States of America

    2 3 4 5 6 7 8 9   045   04 03 02 01 00 99 98

Table of Contents

Introduction

Dear Students,

This book uses letters to teach you how to write well. You'll learn
- how to write well in general, and
- how to write the kinds of letters adults really write.

The last two chapters teach a bonus skill—how to write a persuasive essay. This just means how to talk somebody into something. You may already be pretty good at that.

You will also learn:
- how to use the steps of the writing process,
- how to organize your ideas so they are clear,
- how to paragraph,
- how to write sentences that aren't run-ons or fragments,
- how to use some frequently confused words,
- how to get editing and proofreading help,
- how to spell and punctuate some troublesome words, and
- how to write an impressive, final draft.

You will have lots of help. You won't have to work alone, wondering if you're doing it right. At the beginning of each chapter you'll read a story showing how people do what you are about to do in that chapter.

Then, as soon as you have written your rough draft, which is supposed to be messy and have mistakes, you will get help from classmates and friends. You'll give help to classmates, too. You will work with helpers throughout each chapter, and you can check with the instructor at any time.

The Folder or Portfolio

Your school may give you a manila folder or a portfolio. You may also buy one or make one. Your instructor will keep your folder or portfolio in the classroom until you have finished this class. After that, it is yours to keep.

Instructors and possible employers may look at the letters in your folder to see what you can do. If you follow all the steps of the writing process, all your final drafts will be good.

You will be proud.

Sincerely,

Nan M. Phifer
Author of *Glencoe Writing for the Workplace*

Place this page in your portfolio or folder.

Introducing Yourself

Instructors can help you better when they know you. They care more about you and work harder for your success when they see you as a person with goals and problems and worries and hopes.

Below, write an informal letter to your instructor introducing yourself. Your instructor is the only person who will read this letter. It will not be graded, and it will not be put into your folder or portfolio.

_____
Today's date

Dear_____
    Instructor's name

Tell about yourself.

_____

_____

_____

_____

Tell what you enjoy doing.

_____

_____

_____

_____

You may change or skip any of these questions.
Tell about the people you live with. How do you fit in?

_____

_____

_____

_____

Tell what problems you cope with. What difficulties do you have?

_____

_____

_____

_____

Tell about your long-range goals. Include career goals and personal goals.

_____

_____

_____

_____

What are you good at doing?

_____

_____

_____

What is something you would like to do that you can't do yet?

_____

_____

_____

Tell your instructor how he or she can help you.

_____

_____

_____

Tell anything else you would like your instructor to know.

_____

_____

_____

_____

_____
Print your name so it is easy to read.

Tear this letter out of the book. Give it to your instructor.
OR
You can also use this form as a guide if you decide to E-mail your letter to your instructor.
Thanks.

Achievement Record Form for _____

Student's name

(You can tear this record page out. Place it in your folder or portfolio.)

CHAPTER 1
Requesting Employment Information
Date for Class Discussion _____
Credits Earned _____
Proofread Rough Draft _____
Writers' Wisdom _____
Class Discussion _____
Final Draft _____
Bonus _____

CHAPTER 2
Requesting a Letter of Recommendation
Date for Class Discussion _____
Credits Earned _____
Proofread Rough Draft _____
Writers' Wisdom _____
Class Discussion _____
Final Draft _____
Bonus _____

CHAPTER 3
Requesting Job Interviews
Date for Class Discussion _____
Credits Earned _____
Proofread Rough Draft _____
Writers' Wisdom _____
Class Discussion _____
Final Draft _____
Bonus _____

CHAPTER 4
Writing Formal Thank-You Letters
Date for Class Discussion _____
Credits Earned _____
Proofread Rough Draft _____
Writers' Wisdom _____
Class Discussion _____
Final Draft _____
Bonus _____

CHAPTER 5
Writing to Coworkers
Date for Class Discussion _____
Credits Earned _____
Proofread Rough Draft _____
Writers' Wisdom _____
Class Discussion _____
Final Draft _____
Bonus _____

CHAPTER 6
Correcting a Payment Problem
Date for Class Discussion _____
Credits Earned _____
Proofread Rough Draft _____
Writers' Wisdom _____
Class Discussion _____
Final Draft _____
Bonus _____

CHAPTER 7
Requesting a Change at Work—A Mini-Essay
Date for Class Discussion _____
Credits Earned _____
Proofread Rough Draft _____
Writers' Wisdom _____
Class Discussion _____
Final Draft _____
Bonus _____

CHAPTER 8
Responding to a Request
Date for Class Discussion _____
Credits Earned _____
Proofread Rough Draft _____
Writers' Wisdom _____
Class Discussion _____
Final Draft _____
Bonus _____

CHAPTER 9
Writing a Persuasive Letter—An Essay
Date for Class Discussion _____
Credits Earned _____
Proofread Rough Draft _____
Writers' Wisdom _____
Class Discussion _____
Final Draft _____
Bonus _____

CHAPTER 10
Writing a Persuasive, Formal Letter—An Essay
Date for Class Discussion _____
Credits Earned _____
Proofread Rough Draft _____
Writers' Wisdom _____
Class Discussion _____
Final Draft _____
Bonus _____

Chapter 1

Requesting Employment Information

Setting the Stage ....

"Look! This is free!" Mike exclaims.

"What is?" asks Amber.

"This booklet called *Tips for Finding the Right Job.* I bet it could help me. You know my job is not right for me. I need something different. I just don't know what."

"How can you get one of those booklets?" asks Amber.

"All you have to do is send $1.25 to the Superintendent of Documents. It gives an address."

"Well, write for one," says Amber.

"Easy for you to say. You know I'm not good at writing letters."

"Come on, Mike. You can do it! I'll help you. When I took that night class, I learned about letter writing." Amber takes some sheets of paper out of a table drawer.

"I don't need that much paper. This is going to be a short letter," Mike says.

"I know. But you first have to write a rough draft. You can make all your mistakes in the rough draft. Then we'll fix them. Afterwards you can write your good copy on a clean sheet of paper."

"You mean I have to write it twice?" he asks.

"Let's get started. First leave about a two-inch margin at the top."

Starting the Letter

Mike follows Amber's directions for a Modified-Block Style letter with indented paragraphs.

"Write our street address starting at the center of the page. Then under that, write our city, a comma, our state, and then our ZIP code. Also write today's date under that."

Mike writes:

> 4802 Franklin Blvd., Apt. 329
> Cobblestone City, PA 21059
> March 29, 2000

"You also need to write the address where you're sending it," advises Amber. "It goes to the Superintendent of Documents. So write that toward the left edge of the paper. Leave a margin there, too. About an inch."

Mike writes:

> Superintendent of Documents
> U.S. Government Printing Office
> Washington, DC 20402

"That's great, Mike," compliments Amber. "Next, write *Dear Superintendent of Documents.*"

"Do I need to write *Dear?*"

"Absolutely! That's business letter form."

Mike writes:

> Dear Superintendent of Documents,

"Oh, don't forget to use a colon instead of a comma. You know, that's a dot over a dot."

Mike corrects his punctuation. He begins his first paragraph. He indents it.

Mike writes:

> I am writing to order your pamphlet called "Tips for Finding the Right Job." It costs $1.25, so I am inclosing one dollar and a quarter. Please send it to my address.

Mike says, "My return address will tell them where to send the booklet, right?"

"Yes. Now write the word *Sincerely,* and then sign your name. Print your name under your signature."

"How come?" Mike asks.

"So people can read it. A lot of people write so sloppily that no one can read their names."

Mike's rough draft appears next. Read it. Then, circle any mistakes you find. Notice the letter format he used.

The Rough Draft

> 4802 Franklin Blvd., Apt. 329
> Cobblestone City, PA 21058
> March 29, 2000
>
> Superintendent of Documents
> U.S. Government Printing Office
> Washington, DC 20402
>
> Dear Superintendent of Documents:
>
> I am writing to order your ~~pamhlet~~ *pamphlet* called "Tips for Finding the
>
> Right Job." It costs $1.25, so I am inclosing one doller and a quarter.
>
> Please send it to my address.
>
> Sincerly,
> *Michael Johnson*
> Michael Johnson

Proofreading

Amber studies the letter when it is done. "Your letter looks really nice. But the real test is how it sounds."

"What do you mean?" he asks.

"Listen while I read your letter aloud. Tell me how it sounds. If it doesn't sound right, we can always change it." Mike listens while Amber reads his letter to him.

"Your letter makes sense. It tells what you want. It's clear. It sounds polite, too. You know, we could add *thank you* for a last sentence," suggests Amber. Mike writes in *thank you*.

Amber continues, "The content is fine. When you go to your night class, use the computer lab to keyboard your letter. Be sure to use the spelling checker."

The Final Draft

The next evening, Mike keyboards his letter. He remembers to use the spelling checker. It's a good thing, too, because he misspelled *enclosing*, *dollar*, and *sincerely*.

> **Hint:** A spelling checker shows the correct spelling and makes the necessary changes.

Mike prints his letter and reads it one more time to check the margins. He signs his name and tapes a dollar and a quarter to the page. He knows he would have to write a check if he were sending more money. However, he decided to risk sending $1.25 in cash.

Writing the Envelope

At home, Mike uses an erasable ballpoint pen to address an envelope. The envelope looks like this:

Michael Johnson
4802 Franklin Blvd., Apt. 329
Cobblestone City, PA 21508

Superintendent of Documents
U.S. Government Printing Office
Washington, DC 20402

After he mails his letter, Amber tells Mike that he'll probably have to wait a while for an answer. "You know, Mike, I bet they get lots of requests."

Amber is right. Mike waits over a month for his pamphlet. But when it comes, he gets a good idea for a job he'll like better.

You, too, can write for employment information. See the addresses on page 117. Choose one to write a letter to.

Your Turn!

Brainstorm. Gather your ideas. Get ready to write your rough draft on the lines below. Remember, rough drafts are messy and have misspelled words.

_____
your street address

_____, _____ _____
city,   state   ZIP code

_____ _____, _____
month   day,   year

_____
Write the person's first and last names. Or write Public Relations Personnel or
Superintendent of Documents.

_____
name of company

_____
company's street address

_____, _____ _____
city,   state   ZIP code

Write on the solid lines. Make changes on the dotted lines.

Dear _____:
       Use the name or title from the inside address.

Give the reason for writing.-----------------------------------
_____

Request information or pamphlet's name.-----------------------
_____
Tell if you enclosed money and the amount.--------------------
_____

                        _____
                        Capitalize the first letter of the word _sincerely._

                        _____
                        Sign your first and last names.

                        _____
                        Type or print both names underneath.

You've just written the rough draft of your letter. Is it messy? Good! It should be. Did you misspell any words? Don't worry. We'll proofread later. Did you skip lines? Great! You have space to add and change. If you were messy, misspelled words, and skipped lines, you did it right!

Listen to the ROUGH DRAFT

When you hear what you've written, you sometimes hear ways to make it better. You often decide to:
- Add information
- Change words or sentences
- Cross things out
- Rearrange the order

1. Find a partner. Your partner may be a classmate, friend, or any helpful person.
   Ask your partner to sign here:_____

   Partner's signature

   Say to your partner, "Please ignore spelling and punctuation. Don't proofread yet. Just read aloud so I can hear what I wrote."
2. Listen while your partner reads aloud.
3. Revise what you wrote. This will be your chance to:
   add

         take out

              change

                 rearrange

   Make the content, *ideas* you wrote, better.

Remember! Expert writers revise a lot.

4. Make improvements until it sounds clear and complete.

Proofread for PUNCTUATION

Business letters are formally punctuated. Do you have:

	Yes	No
• a comma separating city and state?	___	___
• nothing separating state and ZIP code?	___	___
• a comma separating day and year?	___	___
• a colon after "Dear _____:"?	___	___

 **Remember!** A colon looks like this :

	Yes	No
• a comma after "Sincerely,"?	___	___

Write the FINAL DRAFT

1. Keyboard your letter.
2. Use the spelling checker.
   OR

If your learning center doesn't have computers, then

1. Ask someone to proofread for spelling *before* writing your final draft.

Remember! Don't proofread for yourself. People tend to be blind to their own mistakes.

2. Write a neat, final draft in blue or black ink. An erasable ballpoint pen works well.

Make a copy of your LETTER

1. Show the copy to your instructor.
2. Use the Achievement Record Form to show credit.

> Congratulations!
> You have written your first business letter.
> Now, you're ready to mail it!
> You will need an envelope.

Address the ENVELOPE

1. Use a ballpoint pen so your writing won't smear or fade.
2. Use the lines provided below for the sample envelope.

your first and last names

your apartment and street address

your city, state   ZIP code

name or job of person receiving letter

name of company or organization

P.O. Box, if one is used

street address

city, state   ZIP code

Sign and Mail your LETTER

You may write as many letters requesting things as you wish. For each letter:

1. Write a messy, misspelled rough draft.
2. Listen to your letter as it is read aloud to you.
3. Revise what you wrote. This is your chance to

add

take out

change

rearrange

4. Keyboard and use the spelling checker. Or, use a proofreader for spelling before you write in ink.

Writers' Wisdom

Define the following words:

rough draft _____

_____

content _____

_____

revise _____

_____

proofread _____

_____

colon (make one)_____

_____

final draft _____

_____

Show these definitions to your instructor for credit.

Credit

Discussion Questions

Read the questions that follow. Prepare to discuss them.

1. Why don't you check spelling as you write a rough draft?
2. When you revise, what are the four things you can do?
3. Why is a messy rough draft good?
4. What questions do you have?

A.   Here are Mike's misspellings. Write the correct spelling on the lines.

    1. sincerly _____

    2. doller _____

    3. inclosing _____

B.   Use the following words in a sentence.

    1. personal _____

    _____

    2. personnel _____

    _____

Show your answers to your instructor.
Ask your instructor to ✓ the bonus line for Chapter 1 on your Achievement
Record Form in your folder.

The next chapter will show you how to ask for something that can change your life!

Chapter 2

Requesting a Letter of Recommendation

Setting the Stage

"Kim, if you get the job as a checker, you'll also get good pay and benefits," Ty says.

"I know. I really want this job, but there'll be a lot of competition. I was thinking it might help if I had a letter of recommendation. You know . . . from that restaurant where I worked last year."

"You're right. It sure would!" Ty agrees. "You should write and ask for one. Do you remember the manager's name?"

"It was Susan Foley."

"Well, write to her," Ty suggests.

Starting the Letter

Kim finds a pencil and some paper. She writes:

Dear Miss Foley,

    I am applying for a job as a checker, and I would like to include a letter of recomendation with my application. Would you write a letter for me? You can send it to me at Apt. 506, 2267 Tandy St. Thank you.

Sincerely,
Kimberly Wilson

Kim hands her letter to Ty. "Would you please read this to me? I want to hear how it sounds."

Ty reads Kim's letter aloud to her and then asks, "Kim, how is she going to remember you? She probably hires lots of employees."

"Maybe she'll remember that I was the one who turned off the smoke detector when Eddie burned the cornbread," Kim says.

Ty looks doubtful. "Perhaps you should add a paragraph at the beginning of the letter to identify yourself."

Kim takes back her letter and adds to it. Each time she begins a new paragraph, she indents the first line about an inch to the right. Kim also writes her return address and the date.

The Rough Draft

Apt. 506, 2267 Tandy St.
Greenacres, SC 32207
August 19, 2000

Miss Susan Foley
Scottie's Best Bar-B-Q
891 East Main St.
Greenacres, SC 32206

Dear Miss Foley,

Ty reminds Kim that she should use a colon not a comma.
Kim sighs. "Why?"
"It's the correct business form."
"Oh, OK."
Kim writes:

Dear Miss Foley:

    I worked at your restrant last year from November untill June.

First I ~~am~~ was a waitress. Later I learned how to work the cash register.

I'm the one who turned off are smoke detector siren when Eddie

burned the cornbread. You praised me for allways being on time and

being cheerfull.

    Now I'm applying for a job as a cashier at a discount store.

~~Will~~ Would you please write a letter of recomendation for me? I can be

telephoned at 992-6340. Thank you.

        Sincerely,
        Kimberly Wilson
        Kimberly Wilson

Proofreading

Kim decides not to write her address again because she has already given her return address. She does add her telephone number.

"Ty, how does this sound now?" Kim reads her improved letter aloud.

"Sounds good to me," says Ty.

Kim knows she needs to listen to each sentence to check for run-on sentences. The best way to do this is to read aloud from last sentence to the first, and listen to how each one sounds.

She reads:

"Thank you. I can be telephoned at 992-6340. Would you please write a letter of recomendation for me? Now I'm applying for a job as a cashier at a discount store."

Ty asks, "What are you doing?"

"I'm listening to each sentence to make sure I didn't write a run-on sentence."

Kim continues.

"Now I'm applying for a job as a cashier at a discount store. You praised me for allways being on time and being cheerfull."

Kim reads the entire letter backward. She listens to each sentence. All the sentences are separated with periods or a question mark. They all make sense by themselves.

The Final Draft

At school the next day, Kim stops at the computer lab to type her letter. She uses the spelling checker. Wow! It's a good thing she did! The spelling checker corrects:

untill	to	until
allways	to	always
cheerfull	to	cheerful
recomendation	to	recommendation
restrant	to	restaurant

Kim shows her letter to her instructor, Miss Spinoza.

"Kim, take a look at this." Miss Spinoza points to the word *are*. "In this sentence, you are writing about the smoke detector. You wrote *are smoke detector*. You want to show possession. The word should be *our*. *Our* shows possession, like our apartment . . . while *are* means being. We are in this room right now."

Kim shakes her head. "I know that. I just goofed." She changes *are* to *our*.

Writing the Envelope

Now Kim has a letter she can feel proud of. She signs it. She addresses an envelope, puts a stamp on it, and mails her request.

A Happy Ending

Kim's employer, Susan Foley, remembered her. Ms. Foley wrote a letter saying that Kim was an energetic worker who always arrived on time, paid attention to her work, and was cheerful.

Kim took this letter to a copy shop where she had 15 copies made. Each time she applied for a job, she stapled a copy to the application form. She was hired for a good, new job.

Brainstorm

Gather your ideas. You, too, can do the same thing.

Think of anyone you've worked for.

Have you babysat?

Have you mowed grass?

Did you work for a business?

Have you done volunteer work?

List your past jobs here:

_____

_____

_____

_____

Show your list to a classmate or friend.

_____

Classmate's or friend's signature

Your Turn!..

**Write your rough draft on the lines below. Remember, rough drafts are messy
and have misspelled words.**

_____
your street address

_____, _____ _____
city,   state   ZIP code

_____ _____, _____
month   day,   year

_____
first and last name of last employer

_____
name of business or company. If not a business, then skip.

_____
employer's street address

_____, _____ _____
city,   state   ZIP code

Write on the solid lines. Make changes on the dotted lines.

Dear M __ _____ :
                  Write last name only

Tell when you worked. -
_____
- -
_____
- -
_____

Tell how long. -
_____
- -
_____
- -
_____

Tell what you did.

Indent your second paragraph.

State your request.

Capitalize the first letter of the word *sincerely*.

Sign your first and last names.

Type or print both names underneath.

Listen to the ROUGH DRAFT

When you hear what you've written, you sometimes hear ways to make it better. You often decide to:
- Add information
- Change words or sentences
- Cross things out
- Rearrange the order

1. Find a partner. Your partner may be a classmate, friend, or any helpful person.
   Ask your partner to sign here:_____
   Partner's signature
   Ask your partner or classmate to read your letter aloud to you.
2. Listen while your partner reads aloud. As you listen, pretend you are your last employer. Will your past employer recall you and understand what you are requesting?
3. Revise what you wrote on the dotted lines. This will be your chance to:
   add

   change

   take out

   rearrange

Remember! Read your work aloud backward. Listen for run-on sentences.

4. Make improvements until your draft sounds clear and complete.

Proofread for PUNCTUATION

Business letters have certain punctuation. Do you have:

	Yes	No
• a comma separating city and state?	___	___
• nothing separating state and ZIP code?	___	___
• a comma separating day and year?	___	___
• a colon after "Dear _____:"?	___	___
• a comma after "Sincerely,"?	___	___

Show your proofread rough draft to your instructor for credit.

Credit

Write the FINAL DRAFT

1. Keyboard your letter.
2. Use the spelling checker.
3. Sign it using blue or black ink.

OR

If your class doesn't have computers, then

1. Ask someone to proofread for spelling *before* writing your final draft.
2. Write a neat copy in blue or black ink.

   Printing is OK. Cursive is OK.

   Leave *big* margins at the bottom and sides.

Make a copy of your LETTER

Congratulations!

Would you like a letter of recommendation to use when *you* apply for jobs? If so, make a copy of your letter to save in your portfolio. Address an envelope, sign, and mail the final draft of your letter.

If you've had more than one employer, you could ask for a letter from each one. Then you'll have several recommendations.

Address the ENVELOPE

your first and last names

your apartment and street address

your city, state   ZIP code

(Mr., Ms., Mrs.)
last name of last employer

business name of company or organization

P.O. Box, if one is used

street address

city, state   ZIP code

Sign and Mail your LETTER

If you mail your final draft, put a copy in your folder or portfolio. Show your final draft to your instructor for credit.

Did you notice that for each letter you followed the steps in the writing process? Did you:

	Yes	No
• write a messy, misspelled rough draft?	____	____
• listen to what your letter said and how it said it?	____	____
• revise your letter? Did you		
add?	____	____
move?	____	____
change?	____	____
rearrange?	____	____
• check for run-ons?	____	____
• write a proofread, correctly spelled final draft?	____	____

Good for you!

Writers' Wisdom

Define the following words:

rough draft _____

_____

content _____

_____

revise _____

_____

proofread _____

_____

letter of recommendation _____

_____

final draft _____

_____

run-on sentences _____

_____

Show these definitions to your instructor for credit.

Credit

Discussion Questions

Read the questions that follow. Prepare to discuss them.

1. How do you decide when to start a new paragraph?
2. How do you show you're starting a new paragraph?
3. How far should you indent?
4. Sometimes business letters aren't indented. Are they right? Are you right?
5. How big should bottom and side margins be?
6. Some people are embarrassed to check for run-ons by reading aloud from last sentence to first. Do you feel embarrassed? How can you do this important step without feeling embarrassment?
7. What is the difference between *our* and *are*?

A. Here are Kim's misspellings. Write the correct spelling on the lines.

    1. untill_____

    2. cheerfull_____

    3. allways_____

    4. restrant_____

B. Use the following words in a sentence.

    1. our_____

    2. are_____

Show your answers to your instructor.
Ask your instructor to ✓ the bonus line for Chapter 2 on Your Achievement Record Form in your folder.

You may discover a job you want in Chapter 3.

Chapter 3

Requesting Job Interviews

Setting the Stage ....

Zac and Jason shoot the last basket and bounce the ball. "It's almost time for work. You know, Zac, I'm really sick of frying food!"

"Why don't you get something different? If you hate your job, try to find another. You can do something else."

"Like what?" Jason asks.

"Well, what do you want to do?" asks Zac.

"I'd like to do auto detailing. I know a guy who does that. He polishes, vacuums, and does some touch-up painting to make cars look like new. They even smell new when he finishes with them."

"You can apply," offers Zac. "You could write to some of those companies. Tell them you want to work for them. Ask for an interview."

"I'd have to write a letter," Jason answers.

"You can do that. I'll help you if you get stuck."

"I'll think about it. Meet you here tomorrow."

Starting the Letter

The next day Jason brings more than the basketball in his athletic bag. He also brings a pencil and pad with a messy letter written on the top page.

"Zac, take a look at this," Jason says.

Zac scowls at the letter. "Why did you skip lines?"

"So I'll have room to revise it. How am I going to revise if I've filled up all the lines? Just read it to me, man. Let's hear how it sounds."

Zac reads aloud.

"I want to do auto detailing. I'm good at close work. I used to make models when I was a kid, and I'd paint them exactly right. Everybody admired how good they looked. I'm 23 years old. Good health. I'll have my GED in 3 weeks. Good work habits. I can come for an interview any time monday though wenesday. Bus 84 gose from where I live to automotive strip, so comming and going won't be a problem. I'll call you on monday to ask for an interview."

When Zac finishes, Jason asks him what he thinks about his letter.

"Sounds good to me, Jason. But I have a feeling you should divide it into paragraphs," Zac suggests.

"How?" asks Jason.

"Well, in the first part you tell how good you are at close work. You tell about your qualifications. That should be one paragraph. Start a new paragraph when you shift from telling about your qualifications to coming in for an interview."

"OK. I'll mark where to indent a new paragraph."

Zac adds, "I think it's important to say *thank you*. Put that in your last paragraph."

"OK. What else?" Jason asks.

"The content is OK. Remember when to capitalize. You didn't capitalize *Monday* and *Wednesday*. Days of the week are always capitalized."

"OK. What else?" Jason grins.

"I think you're ready to check the sentences. Read it backward."

"Are you kidding?"

"No. Just read it aloud, sentence by sentence. Start with the last one. Listen to each sentence."

Jason feels silly, but he reads aloud. He comes to the part about the interview. *"I can come for an interview any time Monday though Wenesday. That's a sentence. Good work habits."* Jason continues.

Zac interrupts. "That's not a sentence. Listen to it all by itself. It's not all complete. You wouldn't walk up to somebody and just say, *Good work habits.*"

"OK. I see what you mean," says Jason. He writes in *I have* before *good work habits.* He continues reading. He finds a few more errors and corrects them.

"I think you've got the idea," says Zac. It's what my English teacher used to call a **fragment.** She said we talk in fragments all the time but shouldn't write them, at least not in formal writing."

Jason reads the rest of his letter. Then he says, "I'll type this in GED lab. It'll look a lot better. Besides I can use the spelling checker.

Jason wonders how to address his letter to a business. He looks in the yellow pages of the phone book under **Automobile.** He locates 17 businesses listed under **Detailing.** He chooses one to write to. When he goes to the GED lab, he keyboards his letter.

The Rough Draft

4306 E. 184th St.
East Los Angeles, CA 97409
July 23, 2000

Manager
Super Slick Automotive Detailing
10049 Axel Boulevard
East Los Angeles, CA 97408

Dear Manager:

   I want to do auto detailing. I'm good at close work. I used to make models when I was a kid, and I'd paint them exactly right. Everybody admired how good they looked. I'm 23 years old and in good health. I'll have my GED in 3 weeks. I have good work habits.

   I can come for an interview any time Monday though Wenesday. Bus 84 gose from where I live to Automotive Strip, so comming and going won't be a problem. I'll call you on Monday to ask for an interview. Thank you.

Sincerly,

Jason Monroe

Jason Monroe

Proofreading

Jason is wise to use the spelling checker. It finds and changes:

Wenesday	to	Wednesday
comming	to	coming
gose	to	goes

It also finds that Jason has left the second *e* out of sincer*e*ly—and he thought he had proofread perfectly!

Jason shows his letter to his instructor, Mr. Biglow. Mr. Biglow reads it and says, "Good job, Jason! I'd hire you if I owned a detailing business. Are you going to mail this?"

"Yeah, I hope I really will get a job."

Mr. Biglow rereads Jason's letter slowly and carefully. "Jason, here's something the spelling checker couldn't catch. You wrote Monday *though* Wednesday." It should be Monday *through* Wednesday. The spelling checker couldn't catch this because you did spell *though* correctly. It just isn't the word you want. Make one more printout with that change. Which businesses are you going to send this to?"

The Final Draft

"That Super Slick sounded good to me," says Jason.

Mr. Biglow says, "While you have your letter on disk, send it to more than one business. Just change the names and addresses of the places where you send it."

Jason's eyes widen. "Good idea."

Writing the Envelope

Using the phone book, Jason addresses the next letter. He changes just three lines. It's quick and easy. He writes envelopes and sends letters to all the companies. He now has 17 chances.

Your Turn!..

Brainstorm. You, too, can ask for an interview for a job you'd like to have. List jobs you'd like to have:

_____   _____

_____   _____

Ask two classmates to let you see their lists. Show your list.

_____ _____
Classmates' signatures

Write a messy, misspelled rough draft. You'll fix spelling, punctuation, and paragraphing later.

_____
your street address

_____, _____ _____
city,   state   ZIP code

_____ _____, _____
month   day,   year

_____
first and last name of Manager, Owner, or Personnel Director

_____
capitalized name of business

_____
street address of the business

_____, _____ _____
city,   state   ZIP code

Write on the solid lines. Make changes on the dotted lines.

Dear M____ _____:
Write the person's position or name if you know it

Tell the job you want.

Tell your qualifications.

Tell what you did.

Indent your second paragraph.

Tell when you can come for an interview.

Capitalize the first letter of the word *sincerely.*

Sign your first and last names.

Type or print both names underneath

Listen to the ROUGH DRAFT

When you hear what you've written, you sometimes hear ways to make it better. You often decide to:
- Add information
- Change words or sentences
- Cross things out
- Rearrange the order

1. Ask someone to read your letter to you. Your reader can be a classmate, friend, or any kind, helpful person.

   Ask your reader to sign here:_____

   Reader's signature

2. Next, read your letter aloud to a listener. Ask your listener:

	Yes	No
• Is it clear?	___	___
• Does it give all the necessary information?	___	___
• Would you hire this letter writer?	___	___

   Why or Why Not? _____

   Ask your listener to sign here:_____

   Listener's signature

3. Revise what you wrote on the dotted lines. This will be your chance to:

   add   take out   cross out   change   rearrange

   Check your sentences.
   Sentence by sentence, read *aloud* from end to beginning.
   Listen to each one. Place a checkmark ✓ to show that you have done this.
   Separate run-on sentences. _____ Fix fragments. _____

Proofread for PUNCTUATION

Business letters have certain punctuation. Do you have:

	Yes	No
• a comma separating city and state?	___	___
• nothing separating state and ZIP code?	___	___
• a comma separating day and year?	___	___
• a colon after "Dear _____:"?	___	___
• a comma after "Sincerely,"?	___	___

Show your proofread rough draft to your instructor for credit.

Credit

Write the FINAL DRAFT

1. Keyboard your letter.
2. Use the spelling checker.
3. Sign it using blue or black ink.
   OR
If your learning center doesn't have computers, then
1. Ask someone to proofread for spelling *before* writing your final draft.
2. Handwrite a neat copy in blue or black ink.

   Printing is OK. Cursive is OK.

   Leave *big* margins at the bottom and sides.

Make a copy of your LETTER

Now, make a copy of your letter to save in your portfolio.

Address an envelope.

Sign and mail the final draft of your letter.

Show your work to your instructor.

Address the ENVELOPE

1. Use a ballpoint pen. Your writing won't smear or fade.
2. Use the lines provided below for the sample envelope.

---
your first and last name

---
your apartment and street address

---
your city, state   ZIP code

---
first and last name (or write Director of Personnel)

---
capitalized name of business

---
street address of the business

---
city, state   ZIP code

Sign and Mail your LETTER

If you don't mail your final draft, put it in your folder or portfolio.

Did you notice you used the steps in the writing process again? You

	Yes	No
• wrote a messy, misspelled rough draft	___	___
• listened to what your letter said and how it said it	___	___
• revised your letter	___	___
• checked sentences for run-ons and incomplete sentences	___	___
• wrote a proofread, correctly spelled final draft	___	___

Writers' Wisdom

Define the following words:

paragraphing_____

_____

indent_____

_____

steps of the writing process

_____

_____

_____

_____

_____

_____

complete sentence_____

_____

fragment_____

_____

Show these definitions to your instructor for credit.

Credit

Discussion Questions

Read the questions that follow. Prepare to discuss them with your classmates. Keep your notes in your portfolio.

1. What information should be included in a request for a job interview?
2. How are fragments caught in your writing?
3. Have you ever been interviewed for a job? What happened?
4. How should you dress for a job interview?
5. What are polite things to do and say at an interview?

Bonus

A. Here are Jason's misspellings. Write the correct spelling on the lines.

    1. comming _____

    2. gose _____

    3. wenesday _____

    4. sincerly _____

B. Use the following words in a sentence.

    1. through _____

    _____

    2. though _____

    _____

Show your answers to your instructor.
Ask your instructor to ✓ the bonus line for Chapter 3 on your
Achievement Record Form in your folder.

You've completed three chapters.
You've already learned a lot!

Reread the letters you've written.

Check each box as you read your first, second, and third letter.

You'll learn an important skill in Chapter 4.

Chapter 4

Writing Formal Thank-You Letters

Setting the Stage ....

When Selena meets her friend, Vita, she says, "I'm so happy. I had the job interview!"

"How did it go?" Vita asks.

"Great! I think I got the job! The interviewer, Ms. Tonem, will call me on Wednesday. She was very interested when I gave her my letter of recommendation from my last job."

Vita hugs Selena. "Let me know when you hear for sure. We'll do something special! Did you write a thank-you letter?"

"What for?" Selena asks.

"To thank Ms. Tonem for the interview. It's what you're supposed to do. Besides, it gives you a chance to remind her about your good recommendation."

"I guess I should. And, I probably should write the man who wrote my recommendation too."

Vita agrees. "You really should. He did you a favor."

Starting the Letter

Selena writes some rough drafts. The next day, she shows them to Vita. Vita looks at them and asks, "Why did you skip lines?"

"So I'll have room to revise. Don't you do that?" Selena asks.

"No. I never thought about it," says Vita, "but it's a good idea."

Selena says, "It took a while to get into the habit. I usually mark every other line with an X to help me remember."

The Rough Draft

Vita reads Selena's first letter. As you read, circle any mistakes you find.

781 1/2 Colorado Rd.
Rancheros, TX 79331
September 3, 2000

Mr. Wayne Poseda
Silver Star Motel
6209 Bluebonnet Highway
Rancheros, TX 79332

Dear Mr. Poseda:

I recieved your letter of recommendation, and I want to thank

~~had~~

you for giving you're time to write it. It was very helpful. I ~~have~~ a

I'll

good interview yesterday, and I think ~~I~~ be hired.

Sincerely,
Selina M. Buena
Selena M. Buena

Selena says, "It's only one paragraph. Do you think I should make it two paragraphs?"

"No. You said everything you need to. One paragraph is enough." Vita adds, "I did see one thing, however."

"What?" asks Selena.

"You used the wrong *you're*. These are two different words. The one you used has an apostrophe that stands for the missing letter *a*. It means *you are*. You want the other word. You want *your*. *Your* is called the possessive form. It shows belonging."

Selena writes the correct form above the wrong word.

"Other than that, it looks fine," says Vita.

"OK," says Selena. "What about this one?"

Proofreading

Read Selena's letter. Circle any mistakes you spot.

781 1/2 Colorado Rd.
Rancheros, TX 79331
September 3, 2000

Ms. Sherry Tonem
Svelty Sports Court
293 Rodeo Drive
Rancheros, TX 79331

Dear Ms. Tonem:

I'am writing to thank you for interviewing me for the position of receptionist at Svelty Sports Court. I am the applicant recomended by Mr. Albergo for my dependable work cleaning units at the Silver Star Motel.

At this time I'am taking a business math class at Blue Prairie

Community Collage, and I plan to also study bookkeeping. If you hire

me I'll be an efficient, friendly receptionist for your buisness, and

in the future I hope I can help you with record-keeping.

Thank you for interveiwing me.

Sincerely,
Selena M. Buena
Selena M. Buena

Vita says, "This looks really good. I can't think of anything to add or change to the content. But I'm going to proofread. I notice the way you wrote *I'am*. You have to write either *I am* or *I'm*. Don't use an apostrophe unless you run the two words together and squeeze a letter out. The apostrophe takes the place of the missing letter."

Selena says, "I'm not a very good speller. Are you going to keyboard this in the computer lab?"

"If I have time before class," says Vita.

"I think you'd better use the spelling checker," says Selena.

"OK."

"Thanks, Vita," says Selena.

When Vita uses the computer's spelling checker, it finds and changes the following misspellings:

recieved	to	received
buisness	to	business
interveiwing	to	interviewing
recomended	to	recommended
collage	to	college

The Final Draft

Ms. Tonem received Selena's letter. She was impressed by her enthusiasm and ambition and hired Selena. Selena went on to study business math and bookkeeping. Eventually she was promoted to a bookkeeper position.

Your Turn! ....

Brainstorm. Gather your ideas! You have written a letter requesting a recommendation. Maybe you sent your letter of request and really did receive a letter of recommendation. Write a letter thanking the person from whom you requested a recommendation.

_____
your street address

_____ , _____ _____
city,   state   ZIP code

_____ _____ , _____
month   day,   year

_____
first and last name of recommendation writer

_____
name of businesss

_____
street address where recommendation writer works

_____ , _____ _____
city,   state   ZIP code

Write on the solid lines. Make changes on the dotted lines.

Dear M _____ :
                    last name only

- -

_____
Thank the person for writing a letter for you.

_____

- -

_____
Tell about your efforts.

_____

- -

_____

Capitalize the first letter of the word *sincerely*.

Sign your first and last names.

Type or print both names underneath.

Second ROUGH DRAFT

Pretend you were interviewed. Write to the person who interviewed you.

_____
your street address

_____, _____ _____
city,   state   ZIP code

_____ _____, _____
month   day,   year

_____
first and last name of interviewer

_____
name of business if it has a name

_____
street address of workplace

_____, _____ _____
city,   state   ZIP code

Write on the solid lines. Make changes on the dotted lines.

Dear M_____:
　　　　　　　　last name only

- -
_____

Thank the person for the interview.- -
_____

- -
_____

Write about some of your qualifications.- - - - - - - - - - - - - - - - - - - -
_____

- -
_____

Tell why the job interests you.- -
_____

- -
_____

_____

Capitalize the first letter of the word *sincerely.*

_____

Sign your first and last names.

_____

Type or print both names underneath.

Listen to the ROUGH DRAFT

When you hear what you've written, you sometimes hear ways to make it better. You often decide to:
- Add information
- Change words or sentences
- Cross things out
- Rearrange the order

1. Find a partner.
   Ask your partner to sign here: _____
   Partner's signature

   Say to your partner, "Don't proofread yet. Just read aloud so I can hear what I wrote."

2. Listen while your partner reads aloud.

3. Revise what you wrote. This will be your chance to:

   add

         change

              cross out

                  rearrange

4. Make improvements until it sounds clear and complete.

   This part takes thought. This is the hardest, most important step.

5. Read your revised rough drafts aloud to a listener.

   _____
   Listener's Signature

   Make final improvements to content.

6. Check your sentences.
   Read aloud from last sentence to first sentence.
   Listen to each sentence by itself.

   Separate run-on sentences. _____ Fix fragments. _____

Proofread for PUNCTUATION

Business letters have certain punctuation. Do you have:

	Yes	No
• a comma separating city and state?	___	___
• nothing separating state and ZIP code?	___	___
• a comma separating day and year?	___	___
• a colon after "Dear _____:"?	___	___
• a comma after "Sincerely,"?	___	___

Show your proofread rough draft to your instructor for credit. ☐

Credit

Write the FINAL DRAFT

1. Keyboard your letter.
2. Use the spelling checker
   OR

If your learning center doesn't have computers, then

1. Ask someone to proofread for spelling *before* writing your final draft.
2. Handwrite a neat copy in blue or black ink.
   Printing is OK. Cursive is OK.
   Leave *big* margins at the bottom and sides.

Sign and Mail your LETTER

1. Sign your letter above your typed or printed name.
2. Use a copy machine or printer to copy your letter.
   File the copies in your portfolio.
3. Show your final letter to your instructor for portfolio credit.
4. Mail your final letter.
   OR
   Place your final letter in your portfolio.

You now have model letters that can help you search for a job.

Writers' Wisdom

A. A contraction is a short way to write two words. The word *don't* is a contraction. It takes the place of the words *do not*. The (') is used to stand in for the missing letters. In *don't*, the (') stands in for the letter *o*.

Examples:

Words	**Contractions**
you are	you're
I am	I'm
cannot	can't
would not	wouldn't

Write the contractions.

1. he is _____

2. I will_____

3. do not_____

4. she would_____

B. Have you heard this jingle?

> *I* before *E* . . . except after *C* . . .
> or when *E* sounds like *A* . . . as in
> *neighbor* and *weigh*

Many words follow this rule.
Examples:

v*ie*w   interv*ie*w

rec*ei*ve   c*ei*ling

Try to complete the spellings of the following words using *ei* or *ie*.
1. You are my best fr_____.
2. He left his tractor out in the cornf_____.
3. Do not dec_____ me.
4. I'm writing the Ch_____ of Police.
5. This is my nephew, Aaron, and my n_____, Sarah.

Ask someone to check your spellings. _____

C. Street addresses can be abbreviated or shortened. Here are some examples:

Road	to	Rd.
Street	to	St.
Drive	to	Dr.
Lane	to	Ln.
Avenue	to	Ave.
Boulevard	to	Blvd.

Hint: Abbreviations need a period at the end.

Write your own examples here:

1. Avenue _____

2. Street _____

3. Road _____

Now, look back at the letters you wrote in Chapters 1–4.

	Yes	No
• Did you abbreviate correctly?	___	___
• Did you remember to include periods?	___	___

Show this work to your instructor for credit. ☐
Credit

Discussion Questions

Read the questions that follow. Prepare to discuss them.

1. Why are thank-you letters important?
2. When should thank-you letters follow business letter form, and when can they be casually written?
3. Why is an apostrophe used in a contraction?

A. Here are Selena's misspellings. Write the correct spelling on the lines.

    1. collage _____

    2. buisness _____

    3. interveiw _____

    4. recomend _____

B. Write the *I* before *E* jingle. (You may look back.)

    _____

    _____

    _____

C. Abbreviate the following words.

    1. Street _____   3. Boulevard _____

    2. Road _____   4. Apartment _____

D. Write the contractions.

    1. do not _____   3. I would _____

    2. can not _____   4. he will _____

E. Write a sentence for the following words.

    1. you're _____

    _____

    2. your _____

    _____

    Here are more abbreviations to keep in your folder.

Apartment	Apt.
Court	Ct.
Route	Rte.
Highway	Hwy.

Show your answers to your instructor. Ask your instructor to ✓ the bonus line for Chapter 4 on your Achievement Record Form in your folder.

You'll get along well with a coworker in Chapter 5.

Chapter 5

Writing to Coworkers

Setting the Stage

Kevin and Ahmad sat together one morning on the city bus; "So, how's it going, Ahmad?" asked Kevin.

"Today I got a letter that made me feel good," answered Ahmad. "It's from somebody at work. He heard about my father's death. He wrote me this letter."

Starting the Letter

Kevin reads Ahmad's letter.

January 24, 2000

Dear Ahmad,

I just learned about your father's death. I want to tell you I'm sorry. I remember once you mentioned that your dad had a heart condition. You were concerned about him then.

I hope your mother is doing OK, and I hope you are too. I feel lots of sympathy.

Sincerely,

Chris

Chris

"You know, Ahmad, I would like to write a letter like this to a girl I knew in high school. She married a guy in the military. They had a baby. I heard the baby was killed a couple of weeks ago in a car accident. The baby wasn't belted in. The girl is OK. She was wearing a seat belt. But she was holding the baby on her lap. I guess the baby's head hit the dashboard. I haven't written to her because I don't know what to say. I don't want her to feel worse."

"You should write to her," says Ahmad. "You won't make her feel worse. She'll feel better. She'll know someone cares. Just tell her you're sorry."

"Here comes my stop. Ahmad, I guess I'll write that letter. See you tomorrow."

The Rough Draft

That night Kevin sits down to write. He skips lines so he'll have room to revise. Read his rough draft. Circle any mistakes you spot.

2204 Lincoln Street
Goldengrain, NE 60933
February 12, 2000

Dear Frances:

            meaning
Ive been ~~mening~~ to write to you. I feel really bad about

                              fair
the death of your baby. It does'nt seem ~~far~~ when little

children die.

I wan't you to know I sympathize.

As Kevin continues to write, he hears the doorbell. When he opens the door, his friend Lucy is there. "Come on in. I'm glad to see you. I've been writing a letter and could use your help."

"What kind of letter?"

"It's a sympathy letter to that girl I told you about."

"Oh, the one whose baby died?"

"Yeah. I don't know what else to say. Here, read what I've got so far," Kevin says.

"You can't send this! It is filled with mistakes!" Lucy exclaims.

"Of course it has mistakes! It's my rough draft. It's supposed to. Right now, I'm trying to figure out what to say."

"Oh," Lucy comments.

"I want your ideas about what it says. I need help with content. We'll proofread later. Help me get my thoughts right."

Lucy looks thoughtful. "Well, I don't think it has to be a long letter. You didn't know the baby, so you really can't say anything about the baby. All you can do is sympathize with the mother. Let me read it to you so you can hear how it sounds."

Lucy reads aloud. Kevin decides to leave the content as it is. "Lucy, make some coffee while I read this letter aloud backward to check sentences. I always feel silly doing that, but it does work."

Proofreading

Kevin finds his sentences are OK. He's ready to move to the next step—**proofreading**.

Lucy knows the difference between business letters and personal letters. She says, "Kevin, you have a colon after the *Dear Frances*. That's OK in a business letter, but personal letters use a comma."

She marks over the colon with a comma. She puts an apostrophe into *I've* to show that some letters are missing. The *h* and the *a* of *have* are missing, so Kevin will need to put an apostrophe in their place.

Kevin watches her mark his work and groans, "I knew that. *I've* for *I have*."

"You also used the wrong spelling of *your*. It's spelled two different ways. When you mean *you are*, you use *you're*. Put an apostrophe for the missing letter. But you wanted the possessive spelling *y-o-u-r*, because you said *your baby*."

Lucy scribbles on the bottom of Kevin's rough draft a reminder.

you're = you are

your = ownership

"You're a good proofreader," says Kevin. "Anything else?"

"Yes, the apostrophe in *doesn't*. You should put the apostrophe between the *n* and the *t* where the letter *o* is missing."

"Apostrophes are my main problem," says Kevin.

"Guess so," agrees Lucy, "because you used one where you didn't need to. You wrote *I wan't you to know,* but *want* doesn't need an apostrophe. No letters are missing."

"I see. I should use apostrophes just two times—where letters are missing or to show possession."

The Final Draft

"Right. Now go ahead and write your final draft. It will comfort your friend, Frances. And I think I should write a letter, too. There is a woman at work whose husband is ill. She hasn't been to work for a month. Her husband is very sick. They have two little kids."

Read what Lucy writes. Circle any mistakes you find.

> 2204 Lincoln Street
> Goldengrain, NE 60936
> February 12, 2000
>
> Dear Margie,
>
> We miss you at work. Someone said your husband is ill, wich
>
> is always tough, so we feel concerned and hope everything works out.
>
> Were thinking of you. Let me know if I can do anything to help.
>
> Sincerely,
> *Lucy*
> Lucy

When Lucy finishes her rough draft, she reads it aloud.

"Does she know how to phone you?" Kevin asks.

"No, I didn't think of it. Lucy adds her phone number. Then she reads her letter aloud, backward, listening for run-on sentences and fragments.

"Now, it's your turn to proofread."

"You probably didn't make any mistakes, " Kevin mutters. "Wait, here you misspelled *which*. You wrote *wich*. It needs an *h*."

"Are you sure? That's how I always spell it."

"Well, then you always spell it wrong," Kevin teases. "And you forgot to put an apostrophe in *were*. You want *we are* so it should be *we're*."

"You're a quick learner, Kevin," Lucy praises.

"Thanks. But I've got a good teacher," answers Kevin.

Your Turn! ·····································

Brainstorm. Gather your ideas! Think of anyone you know who has experienced a loss or a grief. The person could have lost a loved one, good health, a marriage, a home or important property, a job, or a pet. If you don't know someone personally, then make up a name and loss. Write your rough draft below.

_____
your street address

_____, _____ _____
city,   state   ZIP code

_____ _____, _____
month   day,   year

      When writing a personal letter, do not write the name and address here.

Write on the solid lines. Make changes on the dotted lines.

Dear _____,
   If you know the person well, write only the first name.

- -
_____
Offer your sympathy.
- -
_____
- -
Offer some type of help.
_____
- -

_____
Capitalize the first letter of the word *sincerely.*

_____
If the person knows you well, sign your first name only.

Listen to the ROUGH DRAFT

1. Ask someone to read your letter to you. Your reader can be a class-mate, friend, or any kind, helpful person.

   Ask your reader to sign here: _____
   Reader's signature

2. After you listen to what you have written, you may wish to:
   - Add thoughts ____
   - Cross out whatever wasn't good ____
   - Change how you said something ____
   - Rearrange sentences ____

3. Now, read each sentence aloud to someone. Read from last sentence to first. *Listen* to each one.
   - Separate run-on sentences ____
   - Fix fragments ____

   Ask your listener to sign here: _____
   Listener's signature

Proofread for PUNCTUATION

Personal letters have certain punctuation. Do you have:

	Yes	No
• a comma separating city and state?	____	____
• nothing separating state and ZIP code?	____	____
• a comma separating day and year?	____	____
• a comma after "Dear _____,"?	____	____
• a comma after "Sincerely,"?	____	____

Show your proofread rough draft to your instructor for credit. ☐
Credit

Write the FINAL DRAFT

1. Keyboard your letter.
2. Use the spelling checker.
3. Sign it using blue or black ink.

OR

If your learning center doesn't have computers, then

1. Ask someone to proofread for spelling *before* writing your final draft.
2. Handwrite a neat copy in blue or black ink.

    Printing is OK. Cursive is OK.

    Leave *big* margins at the bottom and sides.

Make a copy of your LETTER

If you want to mail your letter, make a copy for your folder. Then, address an envelope, and sign and mail the final draft of your letter.

Sign and Mail your LETTER

If you don't mail your final draft, put it in your portfolio. Show your final draft or copy to your instructor for credit. Did you notice that you followed the steps in the writing process again? You:

	Yes	No
• wrote a messy, misspelled rough draft	___	___
• listened to what your letter said and how it said it	___	___
• revised your letter. You		
added	___	___
moved	___	___
changed	___	___
rearranged	___	___
• checked for run-ons	___	___
• wrote a proofread, correctly spelled final draft	___	___

Writers' Wisdom

A. Show what an apostrophe looks like. _____

B. Show what a comma looks like. _____

C. Show what a colon looks like. _____

D. Explain the two most common uses of the apostrophe.

    1. _____

       _____

    2. _____

       _____

Show your work to your instructor.

Get credit for showing your wisdom as a writer. ☐

Credit

Discussion Questions

Read the questions that follow. Prepare to discuss them.

1. Why is it OK to send handwritten sympathy letters?
2. What is the difference between having content edited and having the rough draft proofread?
3. What can you say or do when the person editing content for you starts proofreading instead?
4. What can you say if your editors are insulting or negative?

Bonus

A. Here are Kevin's misspellings. Write the correct spelling on the lines.

    1. wan't _____

    2. does'nt _____

    3. Ive _____

B. Use the following words in a sentence:

> The word *your* shows ownership.
> *You're* stands for *you are*.

1. your _____

_____

2. you're _____

_____

C. Use either *your* or *you're* in the sentences below.

1. Mack told me about _____ plans to look for a new job.

2. I heard _____ getting a raise.

3. Is this _____ school bag?

4. _____ coming with us to the movies.

5. Are _____ letters ready to mail?

D. Use the following words in sentences.

> The word *were* shows something was in the past.
> *We're* stands for *we are*.

1. we're _____

_____

2. were _____

_____

E. Use either *were* or *we're* in the sentence below.

1. _____ best friends.

2. Bells _____ ringing.

3. _____ you at the wrong address?

4. _____ going to the zoo.

5. _____ you going to say something?

6. Tell Cory _____ on the way to the store.

Show your answers to your instructor.

Ask for a bonus on your Achievement Record Form.

Learn how to get a refund in Chapter 6.

Self-Assessment for a Student-Led Conference

Prepare the material that follows for a conference with your instructor.

A. Carefully reread each letter you wrote. Put a check after you have reread each letter.

- Letter requesting employment information ____
- Letter requesting a letter of recommendation ____
- Letter requesting a job interview ____
- Letter thanking interviewer ____
- Letter thanking recommendation writer ____
- Letter to a coworker ____

B. Which letter was easiest to write? _____

Why? _____

C. Which letter did you have the most difficulty with? _____

Why? _____

_____

_____

_____

D. Which letter makes the best impression? _____

Why? _____

_____

_____

_____

E. You are learning a very important skill—how to use the steps of the writing process. You can use these steps outside this class, any time you need to write clearly and accurately. Can you list the steps here? Look back through Chapters 1–5 to help yourself.

_____

_____

_____

_____

_____

_____

F. As you have used this book and the writing process, what improvements can you see in your writing? _____

_____

_____

_____

_____

_____

_____

G. What areas are you still having trouble with?

_____

_____

_____

_____

_____

_____

H. Write a letter to your instructor. Write about the work in class that satisfies you. Write about what bothers you. How can your instructor help you? How can you help yourself? Add anything you'd like your instructor to know about your school work, about your life, or about your feelings.

Dear_____,

_____

_____

_____

_____

_____

I. Your instructor can write his or her response below.

Dear_____,

_____

_____

_____

_____

_____

Chapter 6

Correcting a Payment Problem

Setting the Stage

Jessica sits at the kitchen table, sipping an after-breakfast cup of coffee and writing in her GED workbook. Suddenly the back door opens and Tyler stomps in.

"What happened?" asks Jessica. "Why are you back?"

"My power drill quit working!" says Tyler. "I can't work on the job with a dead drill."

"But you just bought it a couple of weeks ago, "says Jessica. "Take it back."

"That's what I tried to do," says Tyler as he lays his drill on the table. "I drove to that hardware store where I bought it. Jessie, that store went out of business. It's all boarded up."

"How will you get your money back?" asks Jessica. "That drill was expensive."

"I know," says Tyler, "and it's even more expensive to be off my job. I've got to buy a new drill."

Starting the Letter

"Yeah, I guess so," says Jessica. She looks at the drill lying on the kitchen table. "Look at this label." She brushes some mud off. "Here is the name of the company and an address. You can write to them and ask for a refund."

"I'll do it tonight," says Tyler. "Right now I've got to go buy a new drill and get back to work."

The Rough Draft

That evening Tyler sits at the kitchen table with a pad of paper and pencil and writes the following letter:

(You may circle any writing mistakes you spot.)

> 2268 W. Spruce Lane
> Blue Ridge, AK 91524
> May 23, 2000
>
> Manager
> Customer Relations Department
> Solid Steel Tool Company
> Lakeside City, WI 54623
>
> Dear Customer Relations Manager:
>
> I'm writing reguarding a Solid Steel Power Drill I bought at Willy's Hardware Store here in Blue Ridge on April 5. I know the date and price because when I buy something expensive, I save the receipt. Today while I was at my job, the motor slowed down and finaly stopped.
>
> I went to the store where I bought the drill, but that store has gone out of business. Their is a new chain store here now, so today I went their to buy another drill so I can keep my job. I could not wait untill I hear from you.

> With this letter I am sending you a copy of my receipt. I
>
> payed $140.00 for your best quality of drill, so I am realy suprised
>
> it broke down. The label shows it is model #3815.
>
>   Do you want me to send the drill back to you? I don't want
>
> a replacement since I already had to buy one. I want a refund. If
>
> you want to talk with me, telephone me at our cellular phone on site,
>
> (800) 555-5098. I work from 7 to 4, Pacific Standard Time. Thank you.
>
>   Sincerely,
>   *Tyler Crowell*
>   Tyler Crowell
>
> Enclosure

Proofreading

Tyler stands up and stretches. Then he calls to Jessica. "Jessica, would you take a look at this? Would you please read this to me so I can hear how it sounds?"

Jessica takes Tyler's letter and reads it aloud to him.

"What do you think?" asks Tyler.

"This is really good,"says Jessica. You explained the problem and gave all the specific information like how much you paid and when you bought it. You're enclosing proof. You tell exactly what you want them to do, and you tell how you can be reached."

"If you think the content is OK, would you check the spelling for me?"

"Sure," says Jessica. "While I was reading I noticed that you used the wrong spelling of *there*."

"Huh?" says Tyler.

Jessica explains, "*Their* shows ownership, like *their* car, *their* apartment, *their* band."

"*They're* is *they are* shoved together. The letter *a* got squeezed out, so the apostrophe marks the spot—sort of like a gravestone where the *a* got bumped off. *They're* our best friends. *They're* coming to our party. *They're* driving us nuts."

"*There* is used all the rest of the time—*there* is, *there* are, put it over *there*."

"Jessie, you are a goood, gooood teacher," croons Tyler.

"You just want me to keyboard this letter for you, don't you?" grins Jessica.

Tyler's eyebrows lift. "Would you do that for me?"

"I'll do it at the GED lab tomorrow." Jessica smiles.

The Final Draft

The next day, Jessica keyboards Tyler's letter at lunchtime. It looks good on the monitor, but before printing it she uses the spelling checker. Whoops—good thing she did! The spelling checker changes:

reguarding	to	regarding	suprised	to	surprised
payed	to	paid	untill	to	until
finaly	to	finally	realy	to	really

When Tyler gets home, Jessica shows the letter to him and says, "Tyler, you know what we forgot to do?"

"What?"

"Read it backward. You know, read it from the bottom up and listen to each sentence to be sure there aren't any run-ons."

"Oh, yeah," says Tyler. "Give it here. I'll go do that."

"Read out loud," calls Jessica.

"I will," he says, and he does. Tyler hasn't written any run-on sentences. Every sentence is separate and complete. Tyler's letter is ready to mail.

Remember! When you have a problem with products or payments, if you write a letter stating all the facts and telling what you want done, often someone will understand and correct the problem.

Imagine that something you bought is not the way it's supposed to be or that a bill you received isn't correct. If you do have a real problem of this kind, you could write about it.

A helpful form to follow is on the next page.

Write a quick, messy rough draft.

Your Turn!..

Get ready to write your rough draft on the lines below.

_____
your street address

_____ , _____ _____
city,   state   ZIP code

_____ _____ , _____
month   day,   year

_____
name and position of receiver or write Customer Relations Manager

_____
company's name

_____
company's street address

_____ , _____ _____
city,   state   ZIP code

Dear M_____ :
          name or write Customer Relations Manager.

In the first paragraph, identify yourself. Give your account number if you have one. Give product or serial numbers. Give date and place of purchase. Write on the solid lines.

_____

_____

_____

_____

In the next paragraph, state the problem. Tell what happened.

_____

_____

_____

_____

Ask for specific action. Enclose copies of documentation. Keep your originals.

Tell how you can be reached. Include a phone number.

Capitalize the first letter of the word *sincerely.*

Sign your first and last names.

Type or print both names underneath.

Enclosure(s)

Listen to the ROUGH DRAFT

1. Ask a classmate or friend to read it aloud to you.
2. Edit your letter for this important information:

	Yes	No

Did you tell
- what the problem is?   ___ ___
  Ask your reader to explain your problem.
  If your reader can do this, then you were clear.
- when the problem occurred?   ___ ___
- where the problem occurred?   ___ ___
- who you are?   ___ ___
  Include your middle initial. Sometimes billing
  problems happen when names are confused.
- what you are asking to be done? ___ ___

3. Revise your rough draft.
   Make changes on the dotted lines.
   add
           change
                        cross out
                                  rearrange

4. Read your revised rough draft aloud from last sentence to first.
   Listen to each sentence.   ___
   Separate run-on sentences.   ___
   Fix incomplete sentences.   ___

Proofread for PUNCTUATION

Business letters are formally punctuated. Do you have:

	Yes	No
• a comma separating city and state?	____	____
• nothing separating state and ZIP code?	____	____
• a comma separating day and year?	____	____
• a colon after "Dear _____:"?	____	____
• a comma after "Sincerely,"?	____	____

Show your proofread rough draft to your instructor for Credit.

Credit

Write the FINAL DRAFT

1. Keyboard or E-mail (if available) your letter and use the spelling checker or ask *two* good spellers to proofread for spelling *before* writing your final draft.

_____
Proofreader's signature

_____
Proofreader's signature

2. Handwrite your final draft.

Make a copy of your LETTER

1. Show the copy to your instructor and put it in your portfolio.
2. Use the Achievement Record Form for credit.
3. Mail your letter, if you wrote about a real problem.

Writers' Wisdom

Define the following words:

warranty _____

_____

contract _____

_____

enclosure _____

_____

canceled check _____

_____

Show these definitions to your instructor for credit. ☐
Credit

Discussion Questions

Read the questions that follow. Prepare to discuss them.

1. Why is it better to sound reasonable, not angry or threatening when asking about a problem with a product or service?
2. How can you find out the address of the manufacturer, if you want to write about an item you bought?
3. Why should you keep original documents (such as canceled checks, contracts, and warranties) and not send them with your letter?
4. Why should you keep copies of all letters to and from the company?
5. Why should you include your account number if you have one?
6. Why should you sign your middle name or initial with the rest of your name?
7. If you're writing about an item you bought, why should you tell its code number or serial number and the store where you bought it?
8. If your letter is not answered, or if you receive an unfair response, you can call your local Better Business Bureau or a consumer protection agency to ask for help. Where in the telephone book will you find those numbers?

A. Here are Tyler's spelling mistakes. Write the correct spelling on the lines.

   1. payed _____

   2. reguarding _____

   3. suprised _____

   4. untill _____

   5. gauranteed _____

B. They're, Their, and There

   They're means *they are.*
   > Example: *They're* fun to be with.

   Their shows ownership or possession.
   > Example: That's *their* boat.

   There shows location.
   > Example: Let's row it over *there.*

   There also shows existence.
   > Example: *There* are snakes in this water.

   Now you write a sentence for each word:

   1. they're _____

   _____

   2. their _____

   _____

   2. there _____

   _____

Show your answers to your instructor. Ask your instructor to ✓ the bonus line for Chapter 6 on your Achievement Record Form in your folder.

Chapter 7 may help you improve your job.

Requesting a Change at Work—A Mini-Essay

Setting the Stage ....

Jimmy has studied the spring catalog for the local community college. "I sure wish I could take this diesel engine repair class," he tells his wife, Winona.

"Why can't you?" Winona asks.

"Because it starts at 9 A.M. I have to be at the truck stop for work at that time," he answers.

"Maybe you can change your work hours," suggests Winona. "Maybe you can work from noon to 9 P.M."

"I would have to ask Mr. Ruiz. I don't think he likes me. He's always busy. He never stops to listen."

"Write him a letter. You can put it on his desk so he can read it when he's not busy. Tell him you'll be even more valuable to the truck stop if you learn how to repair diesel engines. You would be a benefit to his business."

Starting the Letter

Jimmy agrees, "Yeah, it would be in his own interest to have a gas pumper who can do repairs too."

"Write to him," encourages Winona.

Jimmy writes a quick, messy rough draft, skipping lines. Read his letter. Circle any writing mistakes you spot.

The Rough Draft

P.O. Box 4208
Cottonwood Canyon, NM 87603
August 28, 2000

Mr. Benjamin Ruiz, Manager
Big Y Truck Stop
Hwy. 86 and Carson Rd.
Bodega, NM 87603

Dear Mr. Ruiz:

Im writing to ask for a change in my work hours. I want

to take a class in diesel repair which is given at 9 A.M. at the

community college. If I ~~would~~ could start work at ~~noon~~ none and work

evenings, then I could take this class.

Maybe someone whose now working at night would like

to have daytime hours. I dont want to inconvenence you. I beleive

I will be a benifit to your busnes when I can ~~due~~ do diesel repairs.

I wont sign up for the class untill I hear from you. You can

call me at home at 474-3311 or talk to me at work.

Sincerely,
Jimmy Strongbow
Jimmy Strongbow

After Jimmy finishes his letter, he asks Winona to read it aloud and tell him what she thinks.

Winona reads the letter to him. Then she says, "Jimmy, Mr. Ruiz has a lot of people working for him. I think you should remind him how long you've been there. You should tell him what kind of work you've been doing. He might not have it fresh in his mind. You could remind him in your first, introductory paragraph."

"You're right," says Jimmy. "Just because I know who I am doesn't mean he knows who I am. He's a busy guy." Jimmy writes an introductory paragraph to insert.

I've been pumping gas at the Big Y Truck Stop for eight months, working from 9 a.m. to 5:00 p.m., six days a week. I'm a steady, reliable worker and get along fine with everyone.

Jimmy reads his introductory paragraph to Winona. "How's this?"

Proofreading

"Good," says Winona. "It's a good beginning. Want me to proofread?"

"Sure do," says Jimmy. "Writing has never been 'my thing'."

"Everybody needs proofreaders," says Winona. She rereads the letter and says, "I'm going to put an apostrophe in *I'm* to take the place of the missing letter *a*. I'm also going to stick one into the word *don't* where the letter *o* from *do not* is squeezed out . . . same thing here for *won't*."

"Let's see," she continues, "what else? *Whose!* There are two different words with different meanings. *Who's* stands for *who is*. That's the one you want because you wrote . . . 'someone who is working at night' . . . The other one, *whose*, shows ownership, like '*Whose* cup is this?'" Winona asks, "Where is that little electronic spelling checker we got at the discount store? I want to check some of these words."

Jimmy finds the spelling checker and types in the words Winona wonders about. The spelling checker shows the correct spellings for:

inconvenience	business
believe	benefit

Jimmy writes the correct spelling above the misspelled words in his rough draft.

The Final Draft

"OK," says Jimmy. "I'll write a neat copy in ink just as soon as I read it aloud to check sentences."

"Don't write on the back," says Winona. "Use two sheets of paper if you need to. Remember to leave big margins at the bottom and sides."

"Right. I'll put my signed letter in an envelope, which I'll put on Mr. Ruiz's desk tomorrow."

Discussion Questions

1. What kinds of changes might you request from an employer?

> **Hint:** Your request is your main idea in the second paragraph of your letter!

2. How could the change benefit:
   - yourself?
   - the business?

> **Hint:** The benefits are reasons supporting your main idea!

3. Why is it a good idea to pretend to be the employer when you listen to your letter read aloud?

4. What change might you request from:
   - a landlord?
   - the owner of a business near your home?
   - a neighbor you don't know?
   - a teacher of your child?

5. What is an introductory paragraph? What should be in it?

6. In one sentence, write your request (main idea)._____

_____

7. List the benefits or the reasons that support your request.

_____

_____

8. Show your main idea and the reasons supporting it to classmates.

_____

_____

Your Turn!..

Brainstorm ideas. Discussion is a good way to brainstorm. Discuss the kinds of changes you might ask from an employer. Write your rough draft on the lines below. Here's a form.

_____
your street address
_____, _____ _____
city,   state   ZIP code
_____ _____, _____
month   day,   year

M_____
name of the person you are writing

_____
name of business (if it has a name)

_____
business's street address

_____, _____ _____
city,   state   ZIP code

Write on the solid lines. Make changes on the dotted lines.

Dear M_____
                last name   Add a colon

_____

_____

Introductory paragraph—Identify yourself, give background.

_____

State your request. Give reasons why it will benefit the company and you.

_____

_____

Tell how you can be contacted. Leave a phone number.

_____

_____

_____

Listen to the ROUGH DRAFT

1. Ask someone to read your rough draft aloud to you. Listen to it, pretending to be the person who will receive it.
   Ask your reader to sign here: _____

   Reader's signature

   Ask your reader: Yes   No
   - Is it clear?   ___   ___
   - Is it reasonable?   ___   ___
   - Is it polite?   ___   ___
   - Is it convincing?   ___   ___

3. Ask your reader to write what should be added, taken out, or changed.

   _____

   _____

4. Revise your rough draft on the broken lines.
   cross out
                          rewrite
                                  write in
                                            rearrange

5. Check your sentences. Read them aloud—*backward*—listening to each sentence.
   Separate run-on sentences.   ___
   Fix fragments.   ___

Proofread for PUNCTUATION

Business letters have certain punctuation. Do you have:

	Yes	No
• a comma separating city and state?	___	___
• nothing separating state and ZIP code?	___	___
• a comma separating day and year?	___	___
• a colon after "Dear _____:"?	___	___
• a comma after "Sincerely,"?	___	___

Show your proofread rough draft to your instructor for credit. ☐

Credit

Write the FINAL DRAFT

1. Keyboard or E-mail your letter.
2. Use the spelling checker.
3. Sign it using blue or black ink.
   OR

If your learning center doesn't have computers, then
1. Ask someone to proofread.
2. Handwrite a neat copy in blue or black ink.
   Leave big margins on the bottom and side.

Make a copy of your LETTER (if you plan to send it)

Show the copy to your instructor for credit.

Address the ENVELOPE

Use a ballpoint pen.

Sign and Mail your LETTER

1. If you wrote about a real change, mail your letter.
2. Put your copy in your folder.

Writers' Wisdom

Define the following words:

request_____

_____

benefit_____

_____

identify_____

_____

A. Here are Jimmy's misspellings. Write the correct spelling on the lines.

    1. Im _____

    2. wont _____

    3. beleive _____

    4. busness _____

    5. benifit _____

    6. inconvenence _____

    7. dont _____

B. Write the correct word on the lines below.

    who's = who is   whose = ownership

    Who's coming with us?   *Whose* gloves are these?

    1. Everyone _____ going swimming should take a towel.

    2. _____ dog is this?

    3. I wonder _____ in charge here.

C. Write sentences using:

    who's _____

    _____

    whose _____

    _____

Show your answers to your instructor. Ask your instructor to 3 the bonus line for Chapter 7 on Your Achievement Record Form in your folder.

In Chapter 8, you're going to be somebody else!

Chapter 8

Responding to a Request

Setting the Stage ....

Mr. Ruiz sits in his office at the truck stop reading Jimmy Strongbow's letter. He rings his secretary.

"Maria, I want you to type a letter." Maria comes to Mr. Ruiz's desk. This is her second week on this job. She wants to do well.

"I'll be leaving on vacation this afternoon, Maria. But before I go, I need to leave word for Jimmy Strongbow. Here's his address on this letter he wrote to me. Use it when you write to him."

Starting the Letter

Maria takes Jimmy's letter. Mr. Ruiz begins to dictate.

"Dear Mr. Strongbow, Since I received your letter, I have talked with Ed Klinkton about shifting his work schedule so you can have mornings off. Ed says he would like to do that. He would rather work mornings and be home with his family in the evenings. So, I can accept your proposal."

Mr. Ruiz continues with directions to Maria, "New paragraph. *I have been thinking I should hire another diesel mechanic. If you become skilled, I can promote you to mechanic. You have a good record here of being reliable and getting along well with others."*

"New paragraph," says Mr. Ruiz to Maria. *"I want you to begin the new schedule next Monday. I'll be on vacation, so if you have any questions or problems, talk with the night supervisor, Chuck Bailey. Good luck with your class. I'm glad you're ambitious."*

The Rough Draft

Maria says, "I'll type this for you, Mr. Ruiz." She takes her dictation to the office computer. She sits down and keyboards the letter that follows. Circle any mistakes you spot.

Big Y Truck Stop
Hwy. 86 and Carson Rd.
Bodega, NM 87601
September 8, 2000

Mr Jimmy Strongbow
P.O. Box 4208
Cottonwood Canyon, NM 87603

Dear Mr Strongbow:

Since I recieved your letter, I have talked with Ed Klinkton about shifting his work schedule so you can have mornings off. Ed says he would like to do that. He would rather work mornings and be home with his family in the evenings, so I can except your proposal.

I have been thinking I should higher another diesel mechanic. If you become skilled, I can promote you to mechanic. You have a good record here of being reliable and getting along well with others.

I wan't you to begin the new schedule next Monday. Ill be on vacation, so if you have any questions or problems, talk with the night supervisor, Chuck Bailey.

Good luck with your class. I'm glad you're ambitious.

Sincerely,

Benjamin Ruiz,
Manager

Writing the Envelope

Maria leaves space for Mr. Ruiz's signature. She reads what she typed, addresses an envelope, and then takes her letter to be signed.

Proofreading

Mr. Ruiz reaches out for the typed letter, looks at it, frowns, and says, "Maria, did you use the spelling checker?"

"Uh . . . no, sir," says Maria.

"You misspelled *received*. It follows the *i* before *e* except after *c* rule. The spelling checker would have caught that."

Mr. Ruiz continues reading.

"Here's a mistake the spelling checker would have missed. You confused *accept* and *except*. *Accept* means to take in or approve. 'I *accept* your proposal.' A woman *accepts* her fiancé's proposal of marriage. You can *accept* an agreement or *accept* an apology."

"*Except* means *all but*. I eat all fruits *except* grapes. Everyone came to our party *except* Roberto. I work every day *except* Sunday."

"I see," says Maria. "I'll change it."

"Here's another word you need to change," says Mr. Ruiz. "I should *hire*, not *higher,* another diesel mechanic.

"Oh, I knew that," says Maria. *Higher* means *taller than,* and to *hire* is to give someone a job."

"Right," says Mr. Ruiz. "By the way, here's another one the spelling checker would have caught—*wan't*. *Want* doesn't have an apostrophe. No letters are missing. You were probably thinking of *won't*, which has an apostrophe where an *o* is missing."

Mr. Ruiz continues, "And what's this word *Ill?* You wrote 'Ill be on vacation.' I hope I'm not sick on my vacation."

"I'll put in an apostrophe," says Maria, blushing.

"OK," says Mr. Ruiz. "One last thing. Do you know when to use periods with Mr., Miss, and Mrs.?"

"I guess not," says Maria.

"Use a period if the word is abbreviated. *Mr.* stands for *mister, Mrs.* is an abbreviation for *misses.* We don't put a period after *Miss* because it's not short for a longer word."

"I see," says Maria sighing. "I'll retype this letter."

"Thanks," says Mr. Ruiz.

Your Turn!...

In Chapter 7, you wrote a letter requesting an important change. Now you are going to be the person who received that letter. Put on a different hat. You've just become another person.

Brainstorm

Imagine you're at your desk writing an answer back to you, the person who asked for a change. You are the boss, or landlord, or instructor, or whoever received your last letter.

Decide how you're going to respond. Will you grant the request? Will you deny it and give reasons? You decide. Use the form that follows on the next page.

Write your own rough draft on the page that follows.

_____
your street address

_____, _____ _____
city,   state   ZIP code

_____ _____ _____
month   day,   year

M_____
name of person who signed requesting this letter

_____
street address of that person

_____, _____ _____
city,   state   ZIP code

Write on the solid lines. Make changes on the dotted lines.

Dear M_____:
       Mr., Mrs., Miss., or Ms. Write last name only. Use a colon.

- -
_____
- -
_____
- -
_____
- -
_____
- -
_____

                              _____
                              signature

                              _____
                              first and last names and position

Listen to the ROUGH DRAFT

A. Ask a classmate or friend to read your rough draft aloud to you. Listen for ways to improve it. Ask your reader for suggestions. Ask your reader to sign here:

_____
Reader's signature

B. Revise your rough draft.

add

change

cross out

rearrange

Remember! A messed up rough draft is a good rough draft!

C. Check your sentences.
Read them aloud, backward (from last to first).
Listen to each sentence by itself.

Separate run-on sentences. _____ Fix fragments. _____

D. Revise on the dotted lines.

Proofread for PUNCTUATION

Business letters have certain punctuation. Do you have:

	Yes	No
• a comma separating city and state?	___	___
• nothing separating state and ZIP code?	___	___
• a comma separating day and year?	___	___
• a colon after "Dear _____:"?	___	___
• a comma after "Sincerely,"?	___	___

Show your proofread rough draft to your instructor for credit.

Credit

Write your FINAL DRAFT

Either
1. Use a word processer to write your final draft or E-mail it.
2. Use the spelling checker.
   OR
1. Ask a good speller to proofread for spelling.

_____
Proofreader's signature

2. Handwrite your final draft in blue or black ink.

Show your final draft to your instructor for credit. ☐
Credit

Writers' Wisdom

Define the following words:

promote_____

_____

ambitious_____

_____

final draft_____

_____

Discussion Questions

Read the questions that follow. Prepare to discuss them.

1. What is the difference between revising and proofreading?
2. What are the two times when we use apostrophes?
3. What skills do business managers need?
4. Where can they learn these skills?
5. What skills does a secretary need?
6. Do you think Maria may eventually become manager of the truck stop? Explain your opinion.

A.   Here are Maria's misspellings. Write the correct spelling on the lines.

    1. wan't _____

    2. recieved _____

    3. Mr _____

    4. Ill (for *I will*) _____

B.   Accept = to take in   Except = all but

    I *accept* your invitation.   Everyone laughed *except* Uba.
    Write *accept* or *except* on the line.

    1. I look OK wearing all colors _____ yellow.

    2. He'll try any sport _____ boxing.

    3. I hope you will _____ my apology.

    4. The instructor would not _____ her late paper.

C.   Hire = contract an employee   Higher = up more

    The boss will *hire* Reggie.   The water rose *higher* than the wall.
    Write *hire* or *higher* on the line.

    1. Tom can jump _____ than anyone else on the team.

    2. The manager wants to _____ a nonsmoker.

D. Write a sentence for the following words.

    1. accept _____

    2. except _____

    1. higher _____

    2. hire _____

Show your answers to your instructor. Ask your instructor to ✓ the bonus line for Chapter 8 on Your Achievement Record Form in your folder.

You'll persuade someone in Chapter 9.

Chapter 9

Writing a Persuasive Letter–An Essay

Setting the Stage ....

Private William Jones is in boot camp. He sits on his bunk writing a letter to his wife. Read his letter. Circle any writing mistakes you spot.

The Rough Draft

April 14, 2000

Dear LaTisha,

    Your news makes me so happy! After you phoned, I told all the guys that I'm going to be a father! I hardly slept at all last night. You'd think I'm the one who is going to have the baby. I'm going to help you take care of him and as soon as he's old enough, take him to ball games and stuff. The guys here slap me on the back and say, "Congradulations!"

    Honey, a while back I was looking at a magazine in the mess hall that had this article about babies of mothers who smoke. It said they are kind of like little runts. They don't get enough oxygen and the nicotine does something bad to their brains and their bodies. They're born smaller than other babies.

LaTisha, I want our baby to be big and smart. I know quitting smoking is really hard, and you've been smoking for a long time. Hon, for our baby, and for me to, I want you to quit smoking. I am so happy, but I am worried to.

The article said the babies of smoking mothers are more likely to be born early, while they're still lightweight, and then they're sick a lot. Some of them even die. Some are born dead.

These puny babies often have learning problems later when they get into school. LaTisha, you are so smart. If we have a girl, I want her to be smart like you. Please don't smoke. And you are so beutiful. I want her to look like you. And if it's a boy I want him to be big and healthy like me.

The article said mothers who smoke are more likely to lose the baby while they are pregnat. LaTisha, don't risk losing our baby!

I love you, honey. Can you do this for me? I want our child to be OK and I want you to be OK to. Everybody knows smoking causes lung cancer and heart attacks, but I saw something really ugly from a TV program. Smoking can cause colon cancer to. (If you don't know what your colon is, just ask your mama. Anyway, the doctors cut it out, and then you have to wear a bag on the outside.)

Do everything you can to stay healthy for me. Eat good food, get a good night's sleep, and please, please quit smoking! You are my wife and my best freind. I want you and our baby to be healthy.

Love,

William

William wonders if his letter will persuade LaTisha to quit smoking. He brings his letter and a pencil and goes outside to find his friend, Jordan.

"How's it going, man?" William asks Jordan.

"OK. How's it with you?"

"I just wrote a letter to LaTisha. I want her to quit smoking."

Jordan says, "Good luck. Lots of people want to quit."

"I know. It's tough," agrees William. "Would you look at my letter? See what you think. Will I make her angry? Read it out loud so I can hear how it sounds."

Jordan reads William's letter aloud.

"What do you think?" asks William.

"I don't see why it would make her mad. You tell her you love her. You give her lots of reasons why she should quit. You're pretty persuasive," says Jordan.

"First of all, is my point clear? Is she sure to understand what I'm getting at?"

"Sure!" says Jordan. "You want her to quit smoking. You say that in the early part after you mention the magazine article, and you repeat it big toward the end. She can't miss your main idea."

"Do the reasons seem convincing?" asks William.

"Yeah, I think so. You give her a bunch of facts. Nicotine stunts the baby's growth before it's born. The newborns are smaller and sicker, and they don't do so well later in school. Then you throw her that punch about colon cancer. Man, that would be gross!"

Proofreading

William says, "LaTisha's a good writer, and I'm not so great. Would you just proofread to see if I made some mistakes? I want her to think about *what* I'm saying, instead of noticing my mistakes."

"Sure," says Jordan. "I'm a good speller—I won a spelling bee when I was in the fifth grade. Let's see. Your paragraphing looks good. Where you say *for our baby, and for me to, I want you to quit,* you should change *to* to *too. Too* means *also.* You're saying *and for me also.* Same thing where you say. *Smoking causes colon cancer to.* You mean *also,* so use *too. I am worried to* should be *I am worried too.*"

William says, "I thought *too* means *too much*—like *too late,* or *too expensive,* or *too far away.*"

"It does," says Jordan. "*Too* means *too much* and it also means *also.* It's got two meanings."

The Final Draft

Jordan uses William's pencil to correct the spellings of:

congratulations   pregnant
beautiful   friend

"There you go, buddy. If she quits smoking, think what all you can do with the dollars that have been going up in smoke."

"Tish will find a way to spend them," grins William.

Your Turn!..

Brainstorm. You're going to write a personal letter to a friend or family member. You are going to try to persuade the person to agree with you or do what you want.

You could think of someone with whom you always argue. This may be your chance to change that person's mind.

You may get an idea for this letter by thinking of how you'd like someone to do something differently. How would you change a relative or a friend?

You'll give reasons why that person should agree with you. You'll try to talk someone into doing something or agreeing with you.

Try several ideas. That way you can choose the best.

1. Write the name of the person to whom you are writing on the line:

_____

Main idea _____

_____

Write this idea in a short sentence.

List some reasons that support your idea.

_____

_____

_____

Think of another person or possibility.

2. Write the name of the person to whom you are writing on the line:

_____

Main idea _____

_____

Write this idea in a short sentence.

List some reasons that support your idea.

_____

_____

_____

Share your ideas with a friend or classmate. Hear that person's ideas.

_____
Friend or classmate's name

Remember! Hearing others' ideas often helps you get more ideas. If this happened to you, write your third idea here.

3. Write the name of the person to whom you are writing on the line:

_____

Main idea _____

_____

Write this idea in a short sentence.

List some reasons that support your idea.

_____

_____

_____

_____

_____

_____

You now have a choice of subjects. Use the one you think will make the most persuasive letter. You may decide to really send it. Use the form that follows to write your rough draft.

Hint: In personal letters, you can leave out full names and addresses.

Dear_____
Write first name only. In personal letters, use a comma here.

Write on the solid lines. Make changes on the dotted lines.

Your opening paragraph should give background. Explain what is happening.

Now make your main point.

Give more reasons.

Concluding Paragraph: Repeat your main idea. Remind the reader of the point you're making.
Summarize your reasons, if you wish. Talk to your reader as if you were with that person.

signature

Listen to the ROUGH DRAFT

You did it! How does it sound?

A. Ask a classmate or friend to read your rough draft aloud to you.

Ask your reader to sign here:_____
Reader's signature

B. If you hear things you want to change, change them now. Ask your reader to write answers to these questions. This person will act as your editor.

    1. What was good about this letter? _____

    _____

    2. Is the main point clear? Yes ___ or No ___ Write the main point in your own words.

    Main point: _____

    3. Underline the main point near the beginning of the letter.

    4. Underline the main point near the end of the letter.

    5. List the reasons the writer used to support the main point.

    _____

    _____

    6. Put a question mark by any of the reasons you think may be wrong.

    7. Give additional reasons that the writer could use.

    _____

    _____

    8. Did the writer persuade you to agree with the main point? Yes or No? If the writer did not persuade you, explain why.

    _____

    _____

    _____

    9. You have just edited for the writer. Good editing isn't easy. It takes thought and work, but—good editing can really help the writer to revise.

C. Revise your rough draft. Good revision takes time.

    1. Read how your editor answered the 9 questions. ____

    2. Rewrite the main point to be more clear, if you can. ____
       Use the skipped, broken lines.

    3. Add reasons your editor suggested, if you like them. ____
       Use notebook paper, skipping lines.

    4. Cross out any reasons you used that you no longer like. ____

    5. You may now have changed, added, and taken out. ____
       Rearrange paragraphs or sentences, if you wish.
       You have now revised. Terrific!
       Careful revision makes a big improvement.

D. Read *aloud* sentence by sentence, from last to first. *Listen* to each one.

    Separate run-on sentences. ____ Fix fragments. ____

Write the FINAL DRAFT

    1. Keyboard your letter.
    2. Use the spelling checker.
    3. Or ask someone to proofread for spelling. _____
                                 Proofreader's signature
    4. Handwrite your final draft.
    5. If you plan to mail your letter, make a copy of it.
    6. Show the copy to your instructor for a grade or credit.
    7. Use the Achievement Record form.

You've just written an essay. Wow! So what's an essay?

A persuasive essay tells your opinion and gives reasons why. You did that. Your main idea was your opinion. The sentence saying your main idea is called a *thesis*. You wrote a thesis.

The thesis is stated near the beginning and is repeated near the end. Your reader finds out soon what your main idea is—and toward the end is reminded what it is. Did you do that?

The thesis is supported by reasons. You did that too. You explained the reasons. You probably gave examples.

Congratulations on writing an essay!

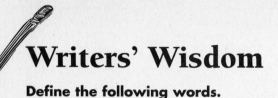

Writers' Wisdom

Define the following words.

editor_____

_____

thesis_____

_____

Discussion Questions

Read the questions that follow. Prepare to discuss them.

1. What does an editor do? How can a good editor help the writer revise?
2. What is the difference between an editor and a proofreader?
3. What should be in an introductory paragraph?
4. What should be in a concluding paragraph?
5. Where should the thesis be located?
6. Exchange your letter for the letter of a classmate. Everyone should trade letters. Without naming the writer of the letter you're holding, read it to the class.

   Discuss these things about each letter:
   - What do you like about this letter?
   - What is its thesis?
   - If this letter came to you, would you be persuaded by it? Why, or why not?

   Return the letter you've read to its writer.

A.   Here are William's misspellings. Write the correct spelling on the lines.

1. pregnat_____

2. beutiful_____

3. freind_____

4. congradulations_____

B.   Write a sentence using the word *too* when it means *also*.

_____

_____

C.   Write a sentence using the word *too* when it means *too much*.

_____

_____

Show your answers to your instructor. Ask your instructor to ✓ the bonus line for Chapter 9 on your Achievement Record Form in your folder.

Only one more chapter to complete.
It's an essay in a formal, business letter.
You know how to write an essay and a business letter, so you can do it!

Chapter 10

Writing a Persuasive, Formal Letter–An Essay

Setting the Stage ....

Shawna tucks the covers around Randy in his crib. "You sleep tight." She bends down and kisses him. "I love you."

Randy kicks at his covers and chirps, "Dink wata."

"No, you just had water. Time to sleep. Good night."

She turns out the light and goes to the living room where Chris lies on the couch.

Shawna says, "Chris, you know what I heard at work today?"

"What?" Chris yawns.

"That new company on River Avenue has child care for its employees. You can take your kid to work with you. They've got a big, sunny room with toys and little tables and chairs and cribs and nap mats. They serve lunch—even have little toilets and sinks."

"Sounds good," says Chris. "Is it free?"

"No, but it saves the hassle of driving to the baby-sitter and wondering what to do if the sitter is sick. Remember when I didn't go to work because Flora was sick?"

"Yeah," says Chris. "And if Randy got sick, you would be nearby. They could just call you."

"And you know what else? Anna could keep working. She took leave because she wanted to nurse her baby, but if she had him there at work, she could go nurse him on her break."

Chris agrees. "Sounds like a win/win situation for everybody. The company wouldn't lose workers because of babysitting problems, and the workers would have less stress and hassle. Why don't you write to your company's president?"

Starting the Letter

Here is Shawna's quick, messy rough draft:
(You may circle any writing mistakes you spot.)

Dear President Glover:

We would feel a lot less stress and hassle if we could bring our kids to work with us. I have to drive fifteen extra minutes each way to take Randy to his sitter. If she is sick I have to find somebody else, and sometimes I just never get to work.

Also I have a friend who took leave for six months so she can breast-feed her baby. If she could take him to work, she could stay on the job and you wouldn't have to train a new worker.

Proofreading

Chris picks up Shawna's rough draft and reads it. "You're giving reasons here, but I think that you should explain your main idea first. The president doesn't know who you are or what your request is."

"I'm requesting on-site child care," answers Shawna.

"Right," says Chris. "So say that in your first paragraph. Then he'll know what you're talking about. Just add an introductory paragraph."

Shawna writes a paragraph she'll add when she writes her final draft.

"How's this?" Shawna reads her new introductory paragraph to Chris.

(You may circle any mistakes you spot.)

I have worked at Arkansas Feather Products for the past seven months in the pillow department. Today I learned that the new company on the other side of town has a big, sunny room where employees can leave their children. Those employees don't have to worry and hassle about baby-sitters because their company gives on-site child care. I'm writing to ask if we can have child care here at our company.

"Good!" says Chris. "Now he'll know who you are and what it's all about. Next explain your reasons."

Shawna numbers her introductory paragraph #1. The paragraph she wrote earlier will be #2. Now she writes #3.

If we had a child care center here at our company, we could hire people who know a lot about little kids. We might hire people who studied child development at the community collage. They could set up a nursery school and even teach Head Start.

Chris says, "When you write your final paragraph, repeat your main idea."

"Why?" asks Shawna.

"Your letter will pack more punch if you do. You tell your main idea in the first paragraph. Give all your reasons in the in-between paragraphs, and then repeat the main idea at the end. That way the reader can't miss your point."

"OK," says Shawna, and she writes:

I think our company should definately have on-site child care. We employees will be able to do our work better if we don't have to worry about baby-sitting. We won't have to miss work because of sitter problems. We won't have to spend extra time and gas driving to baby-sitters. If you would like to talk to me about this idea, you can find me in the pillow department, or phone me at home at 239-1164 after 5:30. Thank you

Chris says, "I'm sleepy. Let's go to bed. Tomorrow I'll read it to you so we can hear how it sounds."

The next evening, Chris reads Shawna's letter aloud so she can hear it.

896 Myrtle Street
Pinetown, AK 90803
March 13, 2000

President Ronald Glover
Arkansas Feather Products
9925 Clint Boulevard
Pinetown, AK 90802

Dear President Glover:

I have worked at Arkansas Feather Products for the past seven months in the pillow department. Today I learned that the new company on the other side of town has a big, sunny room where employees can leave their children. Those employees don't have to worry and hassle about baby-sitters because their compay gives on-site child care. I'm writing to ask if we can have child care here at our company.

We would feel a lot less stress if we could bring our kids to work with us. I have to drive fifteen extra minutes each way to take Randy to his sitter. If she is sick I have to find somebody else, and sometimes I just never get to work. Also I have a friend who took leave for six months so she can breast-feed her baby. If she could bring him to work, she could stay on the job and you wouldn't have to train a new worker.

If we had a child center here at our company, we could staff it with people who know a lot about little kids. We might hire people who studied child development at the community collage. They could set up a nursery school and even teach Head Start.

I think a busines like ours should definately have on-site child care. We will be able to do our work better if we don't have to worry about baby-sitting. We won't have to miss work because of sitter problems. We wont have to spend extra time and gas driving to babysitters. If you would like to talk to me about this idea, you can find me in the pillow department, or phone me at home at 239-1164 after 5:30. Thank you.

Sincerely,
Shawna Sweeny
Shawna Sweeny

Chris says, "It's clear. You make your point at the beginning and repeat it at the end. You give reasons. I bet he'll answer."

"Thanks, Chris. You're a good editor," smiles Shawna.

"I'm a good proofreader too," says Chris. "Want me to check your punctuation and spelling?"

"Sure," says Shawna as she hands her letter to Chris.

Chris finds only three misspelled words: *college, business,* and *definitely.* He marks them and then says, "Go to it! You're ready to write your final draft."

"One last thing," says Shawna. "I'd better check my sentences."

Your Turn!..

You're going to propose a change that would improve a school, business, agency, or service. The change you'll suggest is your main idea—your thesis.

A. Think of any school you attended. Was there anything wrong with it? What should have been done differently? Write your main idea.

1. _____
   Name of the school

   _____
   should have

   This sentence is your thesis.

2. Write sentences telling reasons why.

   _____

   _____

   _____

   _____

   Each reason can be the first sentence of a paragraph—a topic sentence.

B. Think of a business where you buy something or where you work. How could it be improved? Write your main idea.

1. _____
   Name of the business

   _____
   should

   This sentence is your thesis.

2. Write sentences telling reasons why.

   _____

   _____

   _____

   _____

   Each reason can be the first sentence of a paragraph—a topic sentence.

C. Now think of an agency or a service, for example, a law-enforcement agency, a benefits agency, or a bus service. How could the agency or service be improved? What changes would make it work better?

1. _____
   Name of the agency or service

   _____
   should

   This sentence is your thesis.

2. Write sentences telling reasons why.

   _____

   _____

   _____

   _____

   _____

   _____

   _____

   _____

   _____

   _____

   _____

   _____

   These topic sentences can begin paragraphs.

D. Do you now have three possible main ideas to choose from?
   Share ideas with two classmates.

   _____   _____
   Classmate's signature   Classmate's signature

Which idea may work best in a letter? Choose the best. You may decide to send your letter. Write your rough draft using the form that follows.

Remember! Skip lines and indent. Set each new paragraph an inch to the right.

_____

_____

_____

Hint: Before you begin, if you don't know the name of the principal, owner, chief, director—phone the school, business, or agency and ask.

_____
name of person

_____
name of school, business, or agency

_____
street address

_____, _____ _____
city,   state   ZIP code

Dear _____
                    name of person

Hint: In your first paragraph (introductory paragraph) give background. Tell who you are, what happened, when, where, with whom, how, and why.

_____

_____

_____

_____

_____

Begin each paragraph with a reason. Then explain it.
Describe and give examples.

_____

_____

_____

_____

Indent an inch whenever you begin a new paragraph.

_____

_____

_____

_____

_____

_____

_____

You can use notebook paper for writing more paragraphs. When you write your concluding paragraph: Repeat your thesis. Remind the reader of the main point you're making. Tell how you can be reached.

_____

_____

_____

_____

_____
your name

Listen to the ROUGH DRAFT

When you hear what you've written, you sometimes hear ways to make it better. You often decide to:
- Add information
- Change words or sentences
- Cross things out
- Rearrange the order

1. Ask a classmate to read aloud to you._____

   Reader's signature

   Mark improvements.

2. Ask someone to be your editor and answer these questions.
   a. What is the main idea, the thesis? Who should do what?

   _____

   _____

   b. List the reasons you can remember.

   _____

   _____

   _____

   _____

   c. What is the strongest reason?

   _____

   d. What additional reason(s) could the writer add?

   _____

   e. Find the thesis near the beginning and underline it.
   f. Find the thesis near the conclusion and underline it.
   g. Draw stars where the writer could add description or examples.
   h. Most business letters have a polite tone. Is the letter polite? Yes or No?
   i. Do you think the receiver will be persuaded? Why or why not?

3. Now, read your editor's comments.
   Consider them, and then—**REVISE YOUR LETTER**.
   cross out

   add

   change

   rearrange

4. If you plan to mail this letter, try it out on a listener first.

_____
Listener's signature

Get your listener's suggestions.
a. What is good about this letter?_____

_____

b. What would make it better?_____

_____

REVISE SOME MORE.

5. Read aloud sentence by sentence from end to beginning.
    Listen to each one.
    Separate run-on sentences. _____ Fix fragments. _____

Proofread for PUNCTUATION

Business letters have certain punctuation. Do you have:

	Yes	No
• a comma separating city and state?	___	___
• nothing separating state and ZIP code?	___	___
• a comma separating day and year?	___	___
• a colon after "Dear _____:"?	___	___
• a comma after "Sincerely,"?	___	___

Show your proofread rough draft to your instructor for credit. ☐

Write the FINAL DRAFT   Credit

1. Keyboard or E-mail your letter and use the spelling checker.
    OR
1. Ask someone to proofread for spelling *before* writing your final draft.
2. Handwrite a neat copy in blue or black ink.
    Leave *big* margins at the bottom and sides.
    Write on only one side of the paper.
    You have written a persuasive essay within a formal letter!

Make a copy of your LETTER

1. Show the copy to your instructor for a grade or credit.
2. Use the Achievement Record Form.
    If you wish, sign and mail your original.

Writers' Wisdom

Define the following words. (You may look at earlier pages.)

thesis_____

_____

topic sentences_____

_____

introductory paragraph_____

_____

concluding paragraph_____

_____

persuasive essay_____

_____

Show these definitions to your instructor for credit.

Credit

Discussion Questions

1. What makes a persuasive essay persuasive?
2. Discuss persuasive letters you could write to a landlord, to your boss, to the mayor of your city.
3. Why are polite letters usually used instead of rude letters?
4. Read your own letter, or a classmate's letter, aloud to the class. Listen for:
   - the introduction
   - the thesis
   - reasons in topic sentences
   - examples, explanations, and descriptions
   - the conclusion

Here are Shawna's misspellings. Write the correct spelling on the lines.

1. collage _____

2. definately _____

3. busines _____

Show your answers to your instructor. Ask your instructor to ✓ the bonus line for Chapter 10 on your Achievement Record Form in your folder.

Reflections on Writing Letters

Look through all the letters in your portfolio or folder. Then, answer the questions below.

1. Which letter do you feel most proud to have written? Tell why.

_____

_____

2. Which letter was the most difficult to write? Tell why.

_____

_____

3. Which letter seems most likely to be a usable model in the future? Why?

_____

_____

4. Look at each letter. Tell what you learned about writing that you didn't know before you wrote these letters. Give specific examples.

_____

_____

_____

_____

_____

5. Tell what you felt as you worked from chapter to chapter.

_____

_____

_____

_____

_____

6. Write an informal letter to your instructor making helpful suggestions. What was good about this writing program? What could make it better? Could your instructor do something differently? Could you? Make recommendations.

Thank you. Place this reflection into your folder or portfolio.

May all the letters you will write in the future bring the results you want.

DESCRIPTION	ADDRESS	FEE	SASE*
A booklet, *Tips for Finding the Right Job*	Superintendant of Documents U.S. Government Printing Office Washington, DC 20402	$1.25	No
A booklet, *About Jobs Available With the U.S. Government*	Office of Personnel P.O. Box 52 Washington, DC 20044	Free	No
A booklet, *Tips on Trade and Technical Schools* (No. 24–190)	Council of Better Business Bureaus 1515 Wilson Blvd. Arlington, VA 22209	Free	No
A booklet about apprenticeship training: *Matching Yourself With the World of Work*	Bureau of Apprenticeship & Training U.S. Dept. of Labor 200 Constitution Ave., N.W.; Room N-4649 Washington, DC 20402	$1.00	No
A catalog about consumer information: *Consumer Information Catalog*	Superintendant of Documents Consumer Information Center 5A P.O. Box 100 Pueblo, CO 81002	Free	No
A booklet, *FBI Facts and History*	Publications FBI Headquarters, Room 6236 U.S. Department of Justice Washington, DC 20535	Free	No
A booklet, *Tips on Renting an Apartment* (No. 146)	Council of Better Business Bureaus 1515 Wilson Boulevard Arlington, VA 22209	Free	No

* SASE: self-addressed stamped envelope

Chapter 1

Writers' Wisdom

rough draft—a first quick, messy draft, skipping lines

content—the thoughts, ideas, *what* is being said

revise—to make better by adding, taking out, changing, rearranging

proofread—check punctuation, paragraphs, spelling, capitalization

colon— :

final draft—neat last draft

Discussion Questions

1. We want to concentrate on *what* we are saying—our thoughts and ideas. To check spelling would interrupt.
2. add, remove, rearrange, change
3. It shows that we revised it. We made it better.
4. Questions will vary.

Bonus

A. 1. sincerely
   2. dollar
   3. enclosing
B. 1. personal—private, for one person
   2. personnel—employees

Chapter 2

Writers' Wisdom

rough draft—a first quick, messy draft, skipping lines

content—the ideas, the thoughts

revise—to make better by adding, taking out, changing, rearranging

indent—to scoot about an inch to the right

proofread—check punctuation, paragraphs, spelling, capitalization

letter of recommendation—a letter someone writes to say you would be a good person for a job

final draft—neat last draft

run-on sentences—sentences not separated by punctuation

Discussion Questions

1. You start a new paragraph when you change topics or when you go from one idea to a different one.
2. You begin writing on the line below and indent.
3. You indent about an inch.
4. Business letters don't have to be indented if the writer skips a line between paragraphs, but we will indent all paragraphs in this class so we'll be in the habit of indenting for general writing.
5. Bottom and side margins should be about an inch and a half.
6. Explain what you're doing to anyone listening, or go where you'll be alone.
7. *Our* shows belonging. It indicates something we own. *Are* tells existence.

Bonus

A. 1. until
   2. cheerful
   3. always
   4. restaurant
B. 1. Sentences will vary.
   2. Sentences will vary.

Chapter 3

Writers' Wisdom

paragraphing—grouping sentences about the same topic

indent—to scoot about an inch to the right

steps of the writing process—gather ideas, write rough draft, listen to it, revise, check sentences, have it proofread, write neat final version

complete sentence—a sentence that is all there

fragment—part of a sentence

Discussion Questions

1. Our qualifications: experience and/or training, work habits, health, how we can be contacted should be included.
2. Read aloud from last sentence to first, listening to each sentence.
3. Answers will vary.
4. Wear clean, neat, mended clothing that is neither too tight nor too loose, of the type employees wear who do that job.
5. Say, "How do you do?" Shake hands. Sit when invited. Don't smoke, chew gum, or slouch. Answer clearly and honestly. Thank the interviewer for interviewing you.

Bonus

A. 1. coming
   2. goes
   3. Wednesday
   4. sincerely
B. 1. Sentences will vary.
   2. Sentences will vary.

Chapter 4

Writers' Wisdom

A. 1. he's
   2. I'll
   3. don't
   4. she'd
B. 1. friend
   2. field
   3. deceive
   4. Chief
   5. niece
C. 1. Ave.
   2. St.
   3. Rd.

Discussion Questions

1. Other people expect to receive them and consider failure to write them to be impolite. It's a thoughtful thing to do.

2. For a social occasion like an invitation to a home or a party, they may be casually written. As part of business interactions, they should follow business letter form.
3. An apostrophe is used in a contraction to show that there are letters missing.

Bonus

A. 1. college
   2. business
   3. interview
   4. recommend
B. *I* before *e* except after *c* or when sounded like *a* as in *neighbor* and *weigh*
C. 1. St.
   2. Rd.
   3. Blvd.
   4. Apt.
D. 1. don't
   2. can't
   3. I'd
   4. he'll
E. 1. Sentences will vary.
   2. Sentences will vary.

Chapter 5

Writers' Wisdom

A. '
B. ,
C. :
D. 1. The most common uses of apostrophes are to show where one or more letters, or a number, is missing, and
   2. to show possession, ownership

Discussion Questions

1. Sympathy letters are not business letters.
2. Editing content improves how the content, ideas, will be understood. Information may be added. Confusing sentences may be changed. The writer may rearrange sentences or paragraphs. Words may be replaced by better words.

Proofreading checks spelling, punctuation, paragraphing, meaning of words, and spacing.

3. Ask the person to ignore spelling and punctuation and just react to how the ideas are understandable or confusing or incomplete. Explain that proofreading will be done later.

4. Explain that most people's rough drafts are full of mistakes. You focused on your thoughts while you rough-drafted, which is what good writers do. Explain that you need a patient helper.

Bonus

A. 1. want
   2. doesn't
   3. I've

B. 1. Sentences will vary.
   2. Sentences will vary.

C. 1. your
   2. you're
   3. your
   4. You're
   5. your

D. 1. Sentences will vary.
   2. Sentences will vary.

E. 1. We're
   2. were
   3. Were
   4. We're
   5. Were
   6. we're

Chapter 6

Writers' Wisdom

warranty—a written guarantee of refund or replacement if the product is defective

contract—a binding agreement between two or more persons, usually legally enforceable

enclosure—something sent with the letter in its envelope

canceled check—a check with a signature or stamp on the back that shows the person to whom the check was written has received that amount from the bank.

Discussion Questions

1. The reader is more likely to be sympathetic. The reader will take you more seriously.

2. Read the label. If it came in a container, read all the small print on it. Ask to talk to the manager of the store where you bought it to ask who the distributor was. Phone the distributor to ask for the company's address.

3. You may need those documents later. The company may not return them to you.

4. You may have to write again, and you can tell when you first wrote. Letters from the company are signed by an individual, so you can write back to that person. You can take copies of your letters to a Better Business Bureau or Consumer Complaint Department as evidence of your efforts.

5. Companies can more efficiently help you if they can quickly look up their records of the sale or contract.

6. The company may have confused you with a different customer who has a similar name.

7. The company is more likely to make an adjustment if it understands specifically which model you bought and where you did business. The company may contact the local dealer.

8. You are sending something with the letter. It may be a copy of a document or something else.

9. This varies from town to town. Together in class look in your telephone directory under the name of your town, followed by "Chamber of Commerce." You can telephone your Chamber of

Commerce to ask for the number of the Better Business Bureau. Another way to get the address and phone number of your local Better Business Bureau is by writing to the Council of Better Business Bureaus, Inc., 4200 Wilson Boulevard, Arlington, VA 22203, or telephoning the Council at (703) 276-0100. You can put this information in your portfolio to use in the future, if necessary.

Bonus

A. 1. paid
   2. regarding
   3. surprised
   4. until
   5. guaranteed
B. 1. Sentences will vary.
   2. Sentences will vary.
   3. Sentences will vary.

Chapter 7

Writers' Wisdom

request—ask for
benefit—to help
identify—to name

Discussion Questions

1. You might ask an employer to work a different shift, to work at a different station, to do a different type of work, to change something about the place where you work, to work with a different person, to be promoted.
2. a. You might be happier with the change.
   b. You might be able to perform your job better.
3. You'll find out what kind of impression your letter will make, and you'll discover what is unclear or what you could add to make your letter more persuasive.

4. Answers will vary.
5. The introductory paragraph should identify who you are and what your contact is with the person to whom you're writing.
6.–8. Answers will vary.

Bonus

A. 1. I'm
   2. won't
   3. believe
   4. business
   5. benefit
   6. inconvenience
   7. don't
B. 1. who's
   2. Whose
   3. who's
C. Sentences will vary.

Chapter 8

Writers' Wisdom

promote—to move to a better job
ambitious—willing to work hard
final draft—the last copy

Discussion Questions

1. Revising improves content by adding thoughts, removing ideas, rearranging paragraphs or sentences, changing words. Proofreading checks punctuation, spelling, paragraphing, capitalization, and word choice.
2. The two times we use apostrophes are
   a. to show possession, ownership
   b. to show where letters or numbers are missing.
3. Business managers need an understanding of the business, ability to work with people, ability to speak and write clearly, listening skills, and math skills.
4. They can learn these skills in community colleges, technical or trade schools,

apprenticeship programs, and jobs programs.

5. A secretary needs the following skills: listening, writing, and working with people.

6. Answers will vary.

Bonus

A. 1. want
   2. received
   3. Mr.
   4. I'll
B. 1. except
   2. except
   3. accept
   4. accept
C. 1. higher
   2. hire
D. 1. Sentences will vary.
   2. Sentences will vary.
   3. Sentences will vary.
   4. Sentences will vary.

Chapter 9

Writers' Wisdom

editor—helps improve ideas, organization, sentences, and words
thesis—main idea, usually one sentence

Discussion Questions

1. A good editor listens thoughtfully and then tells the writer first what is good about the writing and then what is unclear or confusing, what could be added, how rearranging might help, what words or sentences to change, what to take out.

2. An editor considers *what* the writer is saying, the content. A proofreader checks to see that the writing follows rules about writing.

3. The introductory paragraph should explain what the letter is going to be about.

4. The concluding paragraph should summarize the main points.

5. The thesis should be the first sentence.

6. Answers will vary.

Bonus

A. 1. pregnant
   2. beautiful
   3. friend
   4. congratulations
B. Sentences will vary.
C. Sentences will vary.

Chapter 10

Writers' Wisdom

thesis—the main idea
topic sentence—sentence giving reasons, often the first sentence of a paragraph
introductory paragraph—first paragraph which leads up to and states the thesis
concluding paragraph—last paragraph which repeats the thesis and summarizes reasons
persuasive essay—an essay that tries to make the reader do something or agree with the writer

Discussion Questions

1. It includes reasons a listener or reader can't deny.

2. Answers will vary.

3. Readers are more receptive to polite letters.

4. Read your own or a classmate's letter to the class.

Bonus

1. college
2. definitely
3. business